When Governors Convene

WHEN GOVERNORS CONVENE

The Governors' Conference and National Politics

by Glenn E. Brooks

The Johns Hopkins Press: Baltimore

Printed in the United States of America by Vail-Ballou Press, Inc., Binghamton, New York

Library of Congress Catalog Card Number 61-10364

This book has been brought to publication with the assistance of a grant from The Ford Foundation.

In memory of my father

Preface

AMERICAN state governors have gone through a po-litical revolution in the last half-century. Once they were political homebodies with few responsibilities or interests beyond the boundaries of their home states. Today they are immersed in policy-making and partisan politics at the national and even the international level.

The center of this national and international activity—and the center of this study—is the national Governors' Conference. This association of governors, founded in 1908, has become today a vigorous and creative institution in American political life. The following chapters deal primarily with the Governors' Conference as a collective body, but the story of the institution necessarily hinges on the individual governors who have given it vitality. Thus the names of Woodrow Wilson, Albert C. Ritchie, Franklin D. Roosevelt, Thomas E. Dewey, and LeRoy Collins, among many others, occupy a prominent place in the chapters that lie ahead.

Three themes are woven into the material. The first is that the governor, as an individual officeholder, has become a new kind of state executive with responsibilities in the federal system as a whole and with a continuing influence in national partisan politics. The second theme is that the Governors' Conference, as an institution, has come to occupy a novel extra-constitutional position in the American political system. The third theme is that the image of governors as militant foes of the national government—and especially of federal programs that touch on state responsibilities—is simply not accurate, for the governors have frequently supported joint federal-state enterprises and extensive national control.

Most of the illustrations in these pages concern overt acts of the governors in national affairs. But the motives for these actions are most likely to be found in the broad context of federal-state relations. For example, if the states fail to provide services in spite of incessant public demands for them, the historical odds are good that the national government will move into the void. This inaction of the states, in its own way, is an influence on national policy. Adlai Stevenson once remarked that there would be less talk about states' rights if there had been fewer states' wrongs. Thus, even governors who follow a do-nothing policy in state affairs still have an ultimate influence on the course of the national government.

Regional associations of governors—the Southern, Western, and New England Governors' Conferences—are mentioned only briefly here in order to give full emphasis to the national organization. The regional associations, however, have national interests worthy of separate study even though much of their work is similar to the work of the national Governors' Conference.

The documentary foundations of this study are the annual reports of the proceedings of the Governors' Conferences. Except for some off-the-record debates and speeches, the governors have faithfully kept verbatim records of their proceedings. Reporters and publishers of the proceedings varied from year to year, but in general the records are reasonably complete.

Personal interviews for the study were conducted in several state capitols, in Washington, and in San Juan, Puerto Rico, at the 1959 Governors' Conference. Frank Bane, former Secretary-Treasurer of the Governors' Conference, furnished valuable information and perspective, as did these former chairmen of the conference executive committee: Governors Millard F. Caldwell, of Florida; Robert F. Kennon, of Louisiana; William P. Lane, Jr., of Maryland; William G. Stratton, of Illinois; and LeRoy Collins, of Florida. Interviews with the following governors also contributed to the study: Governor Cecil H. Underwood, of West Virginia; James T. Blair, Jr., of Missouri; Herschel C. Loveless, of Iowa; and especially Governor J. Howard Pyle, of Arizona, who served as President Eisenhower's Deputy Assistant for Intergovernmental Relations after leaving the governorship. John Perry, Assistant to Governor Collins, and Johnson Kanady, Assistant to Governor Stratton, talked to me extensively about conference activities.

The staff at the Council of State Governments in Chicago, which serves as Secretariat for the Governors' Conference, assisted in many ways. Secretary-Treasurer Brevard Crihfield, Mrs. Catherine Barrum, and Miss Betty Greenberg of the Council staff discussed the conference at length and furnished me with a number of scarce volumes of Governors' Conference Proceedings.

My special thanks go to Professors Malcolm C. Moos and Francis E. Rourke, of The Johns Hopkins University, for their suggestions and help; to the Samuel Fels Fund and the Social Science Research Council for their financial assistance; to Lois Lentz for her typing assistance; and to my wife, Ann, whose quick mind and steadfast typing pushed the manuscript through several stages.

Colorado Springs   Glenn E. Brooks
January, 1961

Contents

"*In brief, we are setting up, outside the sphere of the Federal Congress, a new instrument of political life, national in its character, scope, and intention; an instrument, not of legislation, but of opinion, exercising the authority of influence, not of law.*"

Woodrow Wilson 1910

WHEN GOVERNORS CONVENE

I

The New Breed

THE FORTUNES of politics shift in puzzling ways. In 1960, within hours after the American people had chosen Senator John Kennedy as their next president, political columnists were speculating that the defeated candidate, Richard Nixon, was maneuvering into position to become governor of California in 1962, and from there to make another try for the presidency in 1964. Only two years earlier, in 1958, the election of Nelson Rockefeller as governor of New York had automatically catapulted him into the front rank as a presidential possibility.

Yet at almost the same time, some observers were sounding a death knell for the presidential aspirations of American state governors. *New York Times* columnist Arthur Krock, writing just before the national party conventions convened in the summer of 1960, contended that "a fundamental change in American politics is illustrated by the fact that in 1960 no Governor of a state is a strong contender for the Presidential nomination of either party." In the traditional place of the governors stood several senators, a vice-president, and an ambassador to the United Nations. Senators, he noted, "have a first-hand association, which governors necessarily lack, with the foreign policy issues on which the choice of the next President will turn." [1]

On the one hand there were genuine indications that the governors had slipped in national stature: they were having tax troubles at home; their political mortality rate seemed to be increasing; and they were not serious contenders for the presidency in 1960. Yet throughout the country, leading American politicians still regarded the governorship as a direct corridor to the White House.

In the autumn of 1957, Senator William Knowland, at the peak of his career as Republican minority leader, formally announced that he was leaving his seat in the Senate to make a bid for the governorship of California. This move forced incumbent Republican Governor Goodwin J. Knight to abandon his plans to seek re-election. But Knight went out fighting. The decision of Senator Knowland, he said, was "a hydra-headed bid for the Presidency of the United States." In less hostile tones, the New York Times speculated that Knowland "was trying to get in a position that would be a better stepping-stone to the Presidency." [2] Knowland lost the governor's race and involuntarily retired to private life in the prime of his political career. Yet the episode remains as testimony that some American politicians still think that the governorship is nationally more important than a position of leadership in Washington.

While scholars have pondered and politicians have gambled on the future of the governorships, a central fact has emerged from the fifty American statehouses: the modern governors have become key figures in the swiftly changing

[1] New York Times, June 21, 1960.
[2] Ibid., October 4, 1957.

political system. They are key figures not only in the quad-
rennial tug of war for the presidency but also in the ardu-
ous, day to day political struggle that shapes government
policies and puts them into action. Nor is their policy-
making confined to their home states; the governors have
their hands in national and international affairs to an
unprecedented extent.

A landmark in the political evolution of American governors was the formation of the national Governors' Conference. Theodore Roosevelt decided one day in 1908 that
it would be a good idea—and good politics—to assemble
all the American state governors to discuss some pressing
issues of resource conservation. The energetic President
had his meeting, and it served many of his purposes. But
the meeting had a more enduring significance, for it
prompted the governors to organize their own national
conference.

Initially, the Governors' Conference was little more
than a genial club in which governors could retire once a
year from the daily cares of office. But when depression
struck the nation, the governors were pressed with heavy
new responsibilities, and the need for an effective national organization became more evident. The governors
stepped up the tempo of their national endeavors during
the New Deal and the war years, matching the swift
changes that were taking place in national and state government.

Today, the Governors' Conference operates on a year-
round basis. While the conference also serves as a clearing
house for ideas on state government, it spends much of its
energy on national policies of interest to the states, making
its collective influence felt in the halls of Congress, in the

White House, and, on a few occasions, in foreign capitals.

In every contemporary session of the Congress, well-organized groups of governors, co-operating through the Governors' Conference, appear before congressional committees and work privately to press legislation through the House and Senate. Ordinarily this legislation has some direct connection with state government, but the governors do not observe any rigid limits to their activities in Congress.

On numerous occasions contemporary presidents have appeared before the annual Governors' Conference to speak. Presidents have met with select committees of that body to discuss national and international problems. With increasing frequency the governors have asked for consultations with the presidents to present their special programs for the national government.

Immediately after the elections in November, 1960, over half of the governors representing the Governors' Conference made an extended tour of Latin America. The tour was earnestly designed to improve communication between the people and the leaders of the two hemispheres. A year earlier the executive committee of the Governors' Conference had undertaken an equally bold mission in the Soviet Union, meeting with officials from Khrushchev on down in an effort to foster a better understanding of American purposes.

In short, a new group of American governors—typified at the moment by Nelson Rockefeller, Mark Hatfield, Steve McNichols, and many others—co-operating through their central Governors' Conference, have entered the arena of national party politics and national policy-making. They are involved to a degree that sets them off distinctly from their predecessors of a half-century before.

The formation of the Governors' Conference in 1908 gave the governors their first chance to pool their ideas on common problems. But the problems of 1908 were principally internal state matters—administration of the state budget, prison reform, or land utilization. In terms of the official responsibilities of the governors, the national government was comfortably far away. Sporadic conflicts erupted between the states and the national government, but in the main the functions of the two levels were separate and distinct. To the extent that governors were concerned with national policy, their principal interest was in keeping Washington out of state business.

The individual governors of 1908 were relatively weak. Constitutionally, many of the governors were bound by debilitating restrictions on their authority, their length of service, and their salaries. They often had considerable influence as leaders of their state political parties, but they had difficulty in translating their party power into effective power to govern.

Reflecting the weak position of the governors at the time, the early Governors' Conference was neither a vigorous nor a decisive body. With the exception of the first conference, the annual meetings were leisurely têtc-à-têtes devoted to social courtesies, expansive oratory, and the reading of prepared—and usually arid—papers on traditional problems of state government.

A half-century later, the problems, the governorships, and the Governors' Conference had been reshaped by war, depression, and the New Deal. Many of the issues previously regarded as purely state business became national business, and new problems appeared which were pri-

marily national in scope. Whereas state and national responsibilities had once been relatively simple and separate, policies came to be executed jointly by both levels
of government in an era of co-operative federalism. In
the new era, national policies might have a crucial effect
on state policies. Even international policies began to
have a profound influence on the conduct of state affairs.

State government has grown today into a massive operation, with state expenditures climbing at an astounding
rate, particularly during the postwar period—from about
$12 billion in 1948 to $28 billion in 1958. The governors,
presiding over their vast administrative empires, have
held executive responsibilities comparable to those of the
president of the United States.

Along with their new responsibilities, the governors
have won new authority to manage the internal affairs of
their states. Many states have shuffled their executive departments into a compact hierarchy directed by the governor. The professional staffs of the governors have expanded and specialized. Devices such as the executive
budget have given many governors firm command of
their states' fiscal programs. Longer terms, better salaries,
and enhanced prestige have transformed many of the
state governors into genuinely effective leaders.

Part of the new stature of the governors can be attributed to the changes that have taken place in the institution of the Governors' Conference. Discarding its tradition of *laissez faire,* the Governors' Conference today
is a tightly organized, hard-working group committed to
a program of action rather than oratory. Like a chorus in
tune, the collective voice of the governors has been heard

much more loudly and receptively than the discordant sounds of individual governors. Yet the Governors' Conference has not destroyed the high degree of individuality that exists among the state chief executives. While they evidence more uniformity on certain major issues, there is still a healthy abundance of diversity within their ranks.

The national-state problems, the governors themselves, and the Governors' Conference must be viewed as elements in a process of constant interaction. If one changes, the others may change as well, but in ways that defy the inference of simple cause and effect. Changes in the organization and policies of the conference have clearly paralleled the new interest and effectiveness of the governors in Washington. The purpose of these pages is to note some of these changes and to offer, in the final analysis, interpretations of their meaning for the American political process. Specifically, the chapters will move toward the answers to three questions: (1) What is the present role of individual governors, acting either through the Governors' Conference or independently, in the operation of national politics? (2) What is the present status and significance of the Governors' Conference as an institution? (3) How does the activity of the governors in national politics affect the federal system as a whole?

In presenting an analysis of the role of the governors in national policy I have tried to avoid distorting the total picture of national policy-making. Governors are important people, but they must take their place among hundreds of other influential citizens who, through official or unofficial means, help to shape the policies of the United States. The policy-making power of industrial executives, to cite just one group, is probably considerably greater in national affairs than the combined strength of state governors.

There is no question that many groups participate in the formation of public policy. What this study seeks to show is that the governors are no longer stay-at-homes, that they have taken a useful role in national politics and policy-making, and that the nature of state governorships is thereby changed.

In presenting these ideas, I have focused on the collective activities of the Governors' Conference, but in some chapters the emphasis shifts more to the behavior of individual governors. Certainly the governors have not channeled all of their national interests through the Governors' Conference. This is particularly true of the activities of governors in national party politics. Thus, while the Governors' Conference is the principle vehicle for the exploration of how the governors operate on the national scene, there are times when it is useful to depart from the formal conference proceedings to look more closely at the governors as individuals.

2

The House of Governors

IN 1907, a former editor of the *Saturday Evening Post*, William George Jordan, proposed that the governors of the states should band together into a new political institution—he wanted to call it "The House of Governors" —to defend the authority and integrity of the states against the inroads of the national government. As Jordan saw it, the states were losing political power while the government in Washington was expanding dangerously. He believed that the trend could only be checked by the governors of the states acting together.[1]

Under Jordan's plan, all state governors would meet for two or three weeks annually to initiate and inspire ideas for uniform state legislation. The states, in turn, would pass this uniform legislation with increasing regu-

---

[1] Jordan's idea was stated in a brief pamphlet, *The House of Governors: A New Idea in American Politics Aiming to Promote Uniform Legislation on Vital Questions, to Conserve States Rights, to Lessen Centralization, to Secure a Fuller, Freer Voice of the People, and to Make a Stronger Nation* (New York: Jordan Publishing Company, 1907). There had, of course, been previous occasions on which governors had co-operated for some specific purpose. Even in the Revolutionary War the American governors worked together against the British. In the Civil War, groups of Union governors met to assess the course of the war or to chide Lincoln for his military policies. But in every case the governors returned to their separate ways without establishing a permanent organization designed to solve common problems.

larity, and the anticipated result would be that the states would seize the lawmaking initiative away from the national government.

Jordan's proposal for a House of Governors was carefully worded to avoid the impression that it was intended as a constitutionally ordained third house of American government, but the third-house concept was implicit at every turn. The House of Governors was to be a new form of popular representation to supplement the representation of senators and congressmen. Although it was not a lawmaking body, its ultimate objective was lawmaking in the state legislatures. In the author's own words, the House of Governors "should in time become an inherent part in the American idea of self-government and a powerful factor for good in the nation." [2]

For William George Jordan, a House of Governors was the answer to the peril of the union. If he was over-ambitious in his beliefs, if he was naive about the difficulties of getting the states to act in concert, and if his proposals failed to interest the general public, he nevertheless had a fresh idea which was destined to be the cornerstone for the Governors' Conference.

T. R. Takes the Lead

Meanwhile, a restless President of the United States was grappling with a reluctant Congress over one of his most cherished projects, resource conservation. Theodore Roosevelt needed new ways to dramatize his convictions that the government must act forcefully to save the nation's resources from exploitation, for the Congress had

[2] *Ibid.*, p. 6.

not responded with laws or money adequate to satisfy his vision. When a group of his advisors on the Inland Waterways Commission suggested that a conference of governors might be called at the White House to discuss and publicize conservation, Roosevelt pounced upon the idea with customary swiftness and immediately assumed leadership in mapping the conference.[3]

Not only were governors and their advisors invited to attend but invitations were also extended to members of the Supreme Court, senators and representatives of the Sixtieth Congress then in session, members of the President's cabinet, and representatives from sixty-nine organizations interested in natural resources. For good measure, a number of outstanding private citizens were invited as special guests with the result that the conference that met on May 13, 1908, was one of the most august assemblies of public officials in American history. Yet the governors were clearly the center of attention, and the proceedings were designated as a conference of governors without reference to the other participants.

Roosevelt missed no opportunities to further the cause of conservation at the conference. The conference speakers extolled the virtues of conservation while reporters filed reams of copy with their newspapers. With unanimous approval, the assembled governors passed a resolution favoring federal conservation laws and called upon Congress to correct "the waste and exhaustion of the natural resources of the country." [4] Roosevelt also tried

[3] There is no conclusive evidence that William Jordan directly inspired the first conference, but he did serve as an informal secretary to the governors in succeeding conferences. He does, however, deserve the honor of being called the originator of the idea.

[4] Governors' Conference, *Proceedings*, 1908, p. 193. This volume and suc-

his best to whip legislators into line by pointing to the grass-roots support for conservation that was evidenced by the meeting of governors.

Momentarily, the President's propaganda effort failed —Congress still cut off some of his crucial resource appropriations—but in retrospect Roosevelt attached great long-run importance to the first Governors' Conference. "It is doubtful," he said in his *Autobiography*, "whether, except in time of war, any new idea of like importance has ever been presented to a nation and accepted by it with such effectiveness and rapidity, as was the case with this conservation movement when it was introduced to the American people by the conference of governors." As for the resolution passed by the conference, Mr. Roosevelt thought it was "a document which ought to be hung in every schoolhouse throughout the land." [5]

Press reaction to the first Governors' Conference did not entirely reinforce the President's high estimate of the event. *The Nation* was cautious in its appraisal:

> The affair passes into the records not as an epoch-making innovation, not as something that will change our form of government, or even lead to sweeping legislation, but merely as one of those devices to collect and express public opinion and to forward good causes, in which American political genius has always been fruitful. . . . we may be very sure that Mr. Roosevelt had no notion of erecting a new political organism. Certain large plans that he has at heart could be, he felt, furthered by a conference with the executives of the States affected, and they were accordingly

---

ceeding annual volumes will hereinafter be cited as *Proceedings,* with the year and page reference.

[5] Theodore Roosevelt, *Autobiography* (New York: Charles Scribner's Sons, 1958; centennial edition), p. 219.

invited to be his guests. They came, they saw, they were conquered; and now they have gone their way. . . .

Here, then, is no Novum Organon of government, to remove all our political ills. That is not the American way of going to work. We experiment, we tinker, we put on patches; but we do not make all new.[6]

But the *Seattle Times* chose to look favorably upon the potential that was embodied in such a meeting of governors. In an editorial the newspaper observed that a meeting of "forty-four sovereign states under one roof" was "more important in its possibilities than any mere problem of coal, wood, iron, and water can possibly be either within this generation or the next."[7]

The Genesis of Tradition

If Theodore Roosevelt had had his way, future conferences of governors probably would have been called by the president and would have been primarily a means of public support for White House policies. But succeeding conferences pointedly reversed this pattern. Roosevelt left the White House only a few months after the 1908 meeting. His successor, William Howard Taft, felt that the governors should sever their connections with the White House and conduct their affairs entirely on their own.

The next meeting was called by the governors themselves in 1910. At this time President Taft, appearing as

[6] "The Governors at Washington," *The Nation*, Vol. LXXXVI (May 21, 1908), p. 460.

[7] May 15, 1908, quoted in Roy M. Robbins, *Our Landed Heritage* (Princeton: Princeton University Press, 1942), p. 356.

a guest, made clear his intention to stay out of conference affairs. Taft told the governors that it would be better if the conference met in "a neutral place," that is, away from Washington, and "without suggestion from anyone but the Governors themselves." [8] From that time on, presidential control over the Governors' Conference was forgotten.

More important, the governors after the 1908 meeting chose to repress the latent collective power that had been in evidence at the first conference. Once they had detached themselves from the aggressive guidance of President Roosevelt, the dominant faction within the Governors' Conference firmly opposed the creation of a strong, activist group of governors. Most of all they were opposed to the suggestion that the governors should strive to influence national policy, either as a formal instrument of government or as an *ad hoc* pressure group. They also wanted to keep the conference from exercising any coercion over internal policies of state government. Outstanding governors—Augustus E. Willson, of Kentucky; Charles Evans Hughes, of New York; and Woodrow Wilson, of New Jersey—led the state executives in forging an anti-activist tradition for the Governors' Conference that endured for twenty-five years.

The first move of the anti-activist governors was to destroy William George Jordan's theory of the House of Governors. Jordan, who was serving as an unofficial secretary to the conference, had continued to advocate the establishment of a strong but extraconstitutional institution of governors dedicated to decisive collective action.

[8] *Proceedings*, January, 1910, pp. 9–10. The governors held two meetings in 1910—one in January and another in November.

Scarcely had the second conference begun when Governor Augustus E. Willson assailed the concept of the House of Governors. The meeting, he argued, "has no legal authority whatever. . . . It is not a house of Governors. It is simply a conference of Governors." In his way of thinking, the House of Governors idea came dangerously close to sounding like the House of Lords. A conference of governors, on the other hand, should meet only "for the common interest of our people and for the common pleasure of the Governors. . . ." [9]

Governor Willson's attack was reinforced by Governor Charles Evans Hughes. Speaking on the scope and purpose of the conference, Governor Hughes said:

> We are here in our own right as State Executives. We are not here . . . to deal with questions which are admitted to be of exclusively national concern. These are matters to be dealt with by the Federal Government. . . . We are not here to accelerate or to develop opinion with regard to matters which have been committed to Federal power. How the Federal administration shall be conducted is not a matter which concerns State Governors in their official capacity. Whether Congress shall pass a law or not, is for Congress to decide, and with respect to this it is the President's prerogative to make recommendations.[10]

Governor Hughes spoke against the idea that the governors should regard their conference as a third representative institution of government to supplement the House of Representatives and the Senate. Insisting that there was a clear line of demarcation between the responsibilities of the states and the national government, he felt that it would be unfortunate if the governors

[9] *Ibid.*, p. 2.
[10] *Ibid.*, p. 13.

should develop an extraconstitutional body to deal with nationwide questions. Within the spheres of state government, he felt that the conference had a legitimate function of exploring the problems of state executives—but nothing more.

In addition, the Governor of New York sketched out a minimum form of organization for the continuation of the conference which included the idea that the conference "is composed of Executives of brief authority each one of whom is independent of and equal to the others, and upon whom no binding rules can be imposed." [11] He suggested that informal interim committees could handle arrangements for future meetings and programs, and that small donations from participating states would provide for a secretary and minor expenses.

Having laid down the premise that the conference should be severely limited in its influence over constitutional agencies of government and should be highly informal in organization, Governors Willson and Hughes next rejected the use of the device that had been the primary instrument of the 1908 conference—the public policy resolution. One governor implied during the meeting that the conference should pass a resolution on agricultural problems. Governor Willson seized the proposal as a means of attacking the concept of the resolution: "I have a right to say to the Legislature of the State of Kentucky, 'This is the state of affairs that exists and I recommend so and so,'" he said, "But I have not the slightest power or authority, except as every other individual citizen, to tell Congress what to do. . . . The President is the Governor to talk to Congress." [12]

[11] *Ibid.,* p. 21.
[12] *Ibid.,* p. 208.

Most of the governors passively accepted the interpretations offered by the domineering Willson and Hughes. But the combined force of the two men was insufficient to stop a protest led by Governor John F. Shafroth, of Colorado, who believed in a militant role for the Governors' Conference. Governor Shafroth took the floor to warn his colleagues that the federal system stood in jeopardy unless the governors spoke and acted collectively to influence national policies. He observed that the office of governor had dwindled in the eye of the public because the national government was pre-empting traditional rights of the states, while the Governors' Conference afforded the state executives a chance to rebuild their proper dignity.

The activist theories of Governor Shafroth were ignored by the governors without being explicitly rejected. No vote was taken in support of the definitions of the conference offered by Hughes and Willson. No governor rebutted the contentions of Governor Shafroth. No vote was taken for or against any resolution. Instead, the conference leaders merely turned conversation to other issues.

Woodrow Wilson: The Conference Philosopher

While Augustus Willson and Charles Evans Hughes had established the initial course of the conference, it remained for Woodrow Wilson, in his capacity as Governor-elect and later as Governor of New Jersey, to lay out the deeper philosophical implications of the new association of governors.

Although he sided with Augustus Willson and Hughes in advocating an informal, nonactivist conference, Woodrow Wilson saw in the conference new possibilities for the constitutional development of the nation which were ignored by other governors. Addressing the conference as Governor-elect of New Jersey in 1910, he examined the constitutional implications of the formation of the Governors' Conference. "Do we draw together simply as friends," he asked, "or has there arisen in our minds the thought that we have some quasi-constitutional function?" What the Governors' Conference was trying to do, Wilson believed, was to co-ordinate the forces of constitutional vitality which would otherwise be vagrant. "It is an extra-constitutional enterprise," he said, "but natural, spontaneous, imperative, perhaps creative. If it is not constitutional in kind, according to the strict use of that word in America, it is at least institutional."

Wilson's view of the conference as an institution was that it would be a means of co-operation in matters which lie outside the authority of the national government. "In brief, we are setting up, outside the sphere of the Federal Congress, a new instrument of political life, national in its character, scope, and intention; an instrument, not of legislation, but of opinion, exercising the authority of influence, not of law." He carefully qualified his statements to avoid the implication that he wanted to supplant the Congress.

Governor Wilson based his views on his concept of the American federal system. He regarded heterogeneous, self-governing communities as the bulwark of national strength. The preservation of diversity, in Wilson's view, was one of the great tasks of the Governors' Conference. "Our function," he said, "is one of leadership. Leadership, I take it, is a task of suggestion, of adaptation, of the quickening of thought and the devising of means. . . .

Our effort to render this service may result in the setting up of one of those voluntary institutions of counsel by which the life of free countries is enriched, both in action and in opinion." [13]

Despite Wilson's vision of the problems facing the governors, his statement of the purpose of the conference failed to assert the collective nature of any effort that would have to be made to balance national power. Like most of his contemporaries, Woodrow Wilson imagined that the actions of individual governors, inspired by the casual counsel of a social setting, would be sufficient to preserve the stability of the federal system.

The early years of the conference saw the making of a tradition—in a sense, the making of a constitution. The initiative of Governors Augustus Willson and Hughes had successfully established three principles: the conference should be an informal association rather than a deliberative House of Governors with quasi official status in the American system of government; the conference should not attempt to dictate national or internal state policy; and the conference should not resort to public statements of policy on any issues. Woodrow Wilson furnished a philosophic rationale for the association of governors: it was an institution wrought to fill the gaps left by the constitutional growth of the nation. [14]

---

[13] *Ibid.*, 1910–b, pp. 42–48.

[14] In 1912 the conference adopted an informal constitution called the Articles of Organization which tacitly represented acceptance of the anti-activist principles. Article III provided that:

> The functions of the Governor's Conference shall be to meet yearly for an exchange of views and experience on subjects of general importance to the people of the several States, the promotion of greater uniformity in State legislation and the attainment of greater efficiency in State administration.

Nowhere did the articles give the conference machinery for the execution

Why did the commanding group among the governors want to hamstring the authority of the conference? Their own explanations were adequate for the times: existing national and state agencies were sufficiently able to do all the work of governing without interference from a new group. Any move to create a representative House of Governors, even on an extraconstitutional basis, would add unnecessarily to the already complicated system of American government. In their minds it would have been especially inappropriate to create an institution devoted to policy-making through collective action rather than individual initiative.

The governors based their assumptions on the belief that the responsibilities of the states were clearly separate from those of the national government. To an impressive extent they were correct in their analysis of the situation as it existed at the time. Although the national government was moving rapidly into areas formerly believed to be the responsibilities of the states, the nationalization of economic, social, and political issues had not reached its full stride before World War I. While there was active concern about national encroachments, governors felt that

---

of policies. Implicitly, any action resulting from the conference would be the responsibility of individual governors.

To further debilitate the institutional authority of the conference, the articles provided that there would be no permanent president of the conference. A governor would be chosen at the close of every half-day session to preside at the following session. General direction of the conference was placed in the hands of a three-member executive committee to be chosen by the conference. Their terms were for one year, and any vacancies were to be filled by the remaining committee members. For continuity the articles provided for a permanent secretary-treasurer who would serve under the direction of the executive committee. No further organization was con templated. As a final gesture of informality, Article XXI stated that "These articles or any of them may be altered, amended, added to or repealed at any time by a majority vote of all Governors present and voting at any regular annual meeting of the Conference." *Proceedings,* 1912, pp. 71–74

the individual political power of the states was enough to balance national action.

Another factor that made a strong Governors' Conference seem unnecessary was that state government at the time was still highly autonomous and simple in comparison to what it would be at mid-twentieth century. Governors sensed a need to communicate with each other, but they believed that the problems of each state were essentially unique and could not be solved through collective endeavor. In this regard, there were some who knew that a Governors' Conference empowered to influence national policies might also seek to dictate state policies. As a matter of self-protection the governors were not willing to be parties in an institution which could eventually try to tell individual state governments how to run their affairs. In the balance, the possibility of giving up state authority to the Governors' Conference was as undesirable as the possibility of losing authority at the hands of the national government.

The Pressures of Policy

For many years the governors preserved the belief that they were concerned exclusively with state issues in a system divided conveniently into state and national issues. To a considerable extent they did manage to stick to internal state business. The preponderance of Governors' Conference topics between 1908 and 1932, for example, dealt with a governor's administrative authority; the organization and operation of state government; interstate co-operation and comity; uniform state laws; auto, rail, and water regulation in intrastate commerce; prisons and crime regulation; and political practices such as the use of the short ballot and the direct primary.

Reality, however, did not conform to the orderly division of responsibilities cherished by the governors. Rumblings of activity in the national government frequently intruded on the relaxed social calm of the Governors' Conference. Despite their dogged determination to confine their interests to the technical business of state government, the governors found themselves drawn into the vortex of national issues.

When governors discussed state tax programs, for example, they could hardly ignore the fact that the Sixteenth Amendment of 1913 had given the national government revolutionary new taxing powers that could have—and did have—profound consequences for taxation at the state level. Conservation of natural resources also interested the governors, but they could not discuss state conservation measures without recognizing that the national government was moving into the conservation field. Nor could they ignore the fact that extensive national landholdings in the American West affected the economy and government of every state in the area. In agriculture, the governors thought and talked at great length about what the states could do to establish rural credit facilities for farmers, and then watched on the side lines as the national government actually did the job with the passage of the Federal Farm Loan Act in 1916.

The backwash of World War I forced other national issues before the governors. Faced with an upward spiral in prices at the end of the war, the governors sought out President Wilson and Attorney General A. Mitchell

Palmer to discuss joint solutions to inflationary pressures. When a coal crisis gripped the nation in 1919, the governors did not feel adequate to deal with the situation on their own. Instead, they made proposals to the Attorney General and the Federal Fuel Administrator. The states built highways, but the national government made money available for highway construction through a grant-in-aid program. No state road problems could be discussed intelligently without reference to the national grants.

On uncommon occasions in its formative years the Governors' Conference would issue statements or pass memorials concerning national problems, but only under exceptional circumstances. During the twenties, for example, the subject of prohibition crowded its way into conference discussions, and at the meeting in 1923, when the debate over prohibition had boiled into public view, the governors were maneuvered into passing a resolution favoring vigorous enforcement of the anti-liquor laws. This action was taken only after the governors had exhausted every possible means of avoiding a public commitment on the issue.

The Governors in Crisis

Observers of the Governors' Conference in the twenties saw that something was seriously wrong with the organization of governors. The *Chicago Daily News,* observing the 1927 meeting at Mackinac Island, Michigan, called the deliberations "The Governors' Annual Frolic." "To the practical people," editorialized the *Daily News,* "it continues to seem a pity that when so many impressive

State executives meet, nothing much should come of it, except the recurring of occasional remarks. . . ." [15]

The *New York Times* was more critical of the passive attitude taken by the state chief executives. A *Times* editorial writer recalled the original vision of a House of Governors designed to take an active interest in national affairs. Such an institution had "unlimited possibilities for political development," thought the editorialist, but the original concept of the institution had been destroyed. "The yearly meetings . . . have come to be of less and less importance, and to resemble more a gathering of friends assembled for recreation and talk about all things in the heavens above or the earth beneath, without attempting to unite in solemn resolutions for the guidance of the nation." [16]

Meanwhile, the nation gyrated toward governmental and economic chaos. As the twenties drew to a close, it seemed to many that "normalcy" and "prosperity" had triumphed, but beneath the surface of the prosperity were serious signs of disruption. Although business reveled in a policy of light taxation and freedom from onerous regulation, the carelessness of speculation in the stock market was driving the nation's economy to a point of great peril. Agriculture had never rallied from its postwar setbacks, and the efforts of farm leaders to improve agricultural price levels were met with rebuff and veto by Calvin Coolidge, who denounced various reform measures as socialistic government price fixing. Labor fretted under open shops, company unions, picketing restrictions, and yellow-dog contracts backed by a militant use of the

[15] *Chicago Daily News,* July 26, 1927, quoted in *Proceedings,* 1927, p. 182.
[16] *New York Times,* July 26, 1927.

court injunction. Overseas, the Soviet Union was building a new kind of nation, while the Weimar Republic tottered under political and economic burdens.

The collapse of the stock market in October, 1929, and the ensuing depression drove the fortunes of the Governors' Conference to their lowest ebb. During the outwardly prosperous twenties the "Governors' Annual Frolic" was not entirely out of character with the prevailing spirit of the decade. When depression struck, the inability—or unwillingness—of the governors to close their ranks for decisive action was cause for serious concern about the leadership of the state chief executives. A Governors' Conference that could not muster the authority to act in the face of bread lines was no longer a matter for humorous criticism.

Individually, state governors responded to the depression crisis with the few resources at hand. At the outset of the depression, state and local governments were the bulwark of public relief facilities. Governors had general responsibility for the adequate financing and administration of relief programs, and individually pledged their energies and resources to President Hoover.[17] In any accounting of depression measures, individual governors must be given fair credit for a conscientious effort to do something within their jurisdictions.

Yet the measures taken by the individual governors

[17] A devastating drought in 1930 placed the farmers in the Mississippi valley in a serious situation, and governors in the affected states pledged their full co-operation in meeting the crisis. The solvency of thousands of banks was threatened as panic spread among bank depositors, and many governors in the absence of national action, took the initiative in declaring bank holidays to prevent runs on banks. Near the end of President Hoover's term, Governor William A. Comstock, of Michigan, closed the banks in his state for eight days, precipitating a wave of bank holidays on a state-by-state basis.

were piecemeal and inadequate. While the institution of the Governors' Conference stood waiting as a natural instrument for co-ordinating state efforts in the depression, governors went their separate ways without developing a systematic interstate approach to the crisis they faced. Nor did the governors develop adequate means of co-operating with the national government in the early days of the depression. It was quickly apparent that the states lacked financial resources to cope with relief problems and to carry out public works projects demanded by the unemployment situation, but the governors offered no systematic proposals for the solution of their critical financial condition. Finally the national government, acting largely on its own initiative, made temporary loans to the states for relief measures and authorized large additional loans for self-liquidating public construction projects.

While individual governors were performing—as well as they could—to meet the demands of the depression, the Governors' Conference became even less disposed to act. At the 1931 conference, for example, the governors' planning committee avoided practically every topic of urgent concern to the nation. The committee outlawed prohibition as a conference topic. They ruled out water power development, unemployment, and the regulation of public utilities. Their formal program included papers on state supervision of local expenditures, administrative reorganization, veto and extradition, land utilization, and timber resources—all admittedly pertinent topics to the chief executives, but topics chosen for their political insignificance in a period marked by depression and social unrest.

Not all governors, of course, could accept the paralysis

of the Governors' Conference without protest. Four governors in particular—Albert C. Ritchie, of Maryland;
Theodore Christianson, of Minnesota; Gifford Pinchot,
of Pennsylvania; and Franklin D. Roosevelt, of New
York—deserve prominent mention for their attempts to
energize the conference, to make it aware of its national
responsibilities, and to organize it for effective action.

Ritchie and Christianson were primarily concerned
with encroachments of the national government on the
powers of the states. Both were convinced that a collective
effort by the Governors' Conference was necessary to restore the federal balance of power. Roosevelt and Pinchot,
however, were more concerned with the solution of substantive political problems by any level of government
that was most capable of solving them. Whatever their
motives may have been, these four executives tried on
many occasions to goad their fellow governors into action.
This was especially true in 1931, when Roosevelt, Ritchie,
and Pinchot practically commandeered the conference
rostrum in an effort to inject national issues into the
deliberations. "I think it is fair to say among ourselves,"
said Governor Ritchie, "that we, the representatives of
the States, refrain from debating many of those questions
which are the realities of our modern national life." [18]

In the main, the assaults of the activists were unheeded,
and the governors entered the thirties with an attitude of
solemn indifference to national issues. Most state executives of the Hoover era—both Democrats and Republicans—were controlled by a concept of the governorship
which did not admit the possibility of gubernatorial action in national or interstate affairs. Since the birth of

[18] *Proceedings*, 1931, p. 84.

the federal system, the definition of a governorship confined the governors to immediate, internal state responsibilities. State constitutions made no mention of national or interstate responsibilities outside of such minor matters as extradition. This was the concept that dominated the minds of the governors even as the social and economic structure supporting the concept began to change with great speed.

Even if the governors had not been faced with practical barriers to effective national action, it would have been difficult for them to think of themselves in a national role. New ways of action would have been inadequate without new ways of thinking. Until a sufficient number of governors were able to conceive of a new role for themselves in national and interstate policy, the Governors' Conference had little hope of becoming a creative force in the political system.

If the governors lacked the conceptual tools to expand their roles, they also had difficulty comprehending the vast nationalization of public issues brought about by economic and social circumstance. The nation was becoming more homogeneous. Technology was in a state of revolution. Commerce and labor were operating without special regard for state boundaries, and the need for uniform national action—either by the states or the national government—was increasing at a rapid pace. The governors perceived only dimly the depth and permanence of the changes taking place before their eyes. Above all, they did not see themselves as actors in the drama which converted minor provincial problems into major national ones and which made national and international issues germane to state government.

After the depression began, it took them more than a decade to weld themselves into an effective national body. It was a space of years involving another generation of governors, a permanent secretariat, a new kind of national government under the leadership of Franklin Roosevelt, a war, and a share of the normal accidents of politics which changed the course of this institution when it was least expected. This welding together is the subject of the next chapter.

3

Renaissance

SINGLE EVENTS rarely account for revolutions in the behavior of men and institutions. In the case of the Governors' Conference, several stages were involved in the transition from a passive organization into an aggressive institution dedicated to the solution of state, national, and international problems.

The first stage involved the birth of a new national consciousness and a willingness to act on national issues. The change of spirit paralleled the inauguration of Franklin D. Roosevelt as President in 1933. As Governor of New York, Roosevelt had repeatedly voiced his faith in the ability of the states to contribute to the solution of the crucial issues of the depression era. Putting his faith to the test, the new President summoned a conference of governors at the White House on the second working day of his administration. A bipartisan group of twenty governors and eleven governors' representatives attended the meeting. The agenda of the conference included consultation on federal-state relations, relief, public expenditures, and the national banking situation.

Roosevelt made a strong plea to the governors for full co-operation in dealing with the national crisis, knowing well that the tradition of the Governors' Conference was firmly fixed against collective action. Yet the mood of the governors had changed. Spurred beyond their normal reserve by the forcefulness of the President and the excitement of the times, the governors cast aside their traditions and struck out on a new course. Unanimously they resolved that:

> Without regard to our political affiliations we . . . hereby express our confidence and faith in our President and urge the Congress and all the people of our united country to cooperate with him in such action as he shall find necessary or desirable in restoring banking and economic stability.[1]

Three supplementary resolutions dealing with specific policies were also adopted by the governors.

In several respects the 1933 White House conference was a repeat performance of the original 1908 session summoned by Theodore Roosevelt. The meeting was not a plenary session of the Governors' Conference. The governors had not organized the meeting themselves, but had been asked to come by F.D.R. The topics of discussion —unemployment, relief, land use, and banking—had been determined by Roosevelt, and it is likely that the final resolutions adopted by the conference were guided by the President.

The conference also had its strategic considerations. As President, Franklin Roosevelt was in a position to work a double play. By calling the governors together he was rallying public support for his administration. Second, and most important for the governors, Roosevelt was offering the state executives a role in the greatness of the times.

[1] *New York Times*, March 7, 1933.

The President did not regard the governors as feudal barons who had come to do homage to the king. He respected them deeply and sought their counsel. In a radio address to the regular Governors' Conference on July 25, 1933, Roosevelt emphasized that the administration did not intend for the governors to become lieutenants of the national government. The President said he sought to "strengthen the bonds" and "adjust the balance between mutual State and Federal undertakings" such as oil and land regulations.[2]

To the *New York Times,* the attitude of the President meant a potential renaissance for the governors. Recalling that Roosevelt as governor of New York had long sought to find a function "for what, on paper, seems to be one of the most powerful groups in the United States," a *Times* editorial observed that the President's emphasis on mutual undertakings was of great significance for the governors. "There are more of these mutualities than ever before," said the editorial. "Their increase may energize the 'House of Governors' into a body as important as it was originally expected to be. . . ."[3]

The Shock of The New Deal

The harmony of the inaugural period was brief. Both Roosevelt and the governors had started from the premise that the states would be key instruments in national recovery and reform. But the states were slow to respond—or at least that was Roosevelt's impression—and he increasingly relied on the authority of the national govern-

[2] *Ibid.,* July 26, 1933.
[3] *Ibid.,* July 27, 1933.

ment to solve pressing economic and social problems. In all probability that is not what Roosevelt had intended at the outset. By 1935, however, the national government had clearly shifted its emphasis to nationally controlled recovery programs which disregarded the states.

At every hand, the national government experimented with new ideas in federal emergency relief, federal industrial recovery plans, social security, public works, and fiscal regulation. Many of these programs bypassed state governments and dealt directly with individual citizens. Meanwhile, the states stood by, attempting in some cases to develop their own programs, but never quite sure what course the Roosevelt administration would take.[4]

In the face of Roosevelt's aggressive policies, the Governors' Conference was transformed from a staid social club into a forum for the heated discussion of national programs and federal-state relations. Conference agenda in the mid-thirties were devoted almost exclusively to problems of national concern, and the pitch of discussion rose from the dull throbs of the twenties to a new high of intensity.

Some of the governors reacted bitterly against Roosevelt and his innovations. When the President created the Works Progress Administration in 1935, governors discovered that they had been deprived of administrative authority in direct emergency relief and public employment programs. After hearing explanations of the new

[4] In 1935, the governors led a move to establish minimum wage agreements through interstate compacts. With full support of the Governors' Conference, a labor compact conference was held and negotiations were under way. But Congress swept into the field with the passage of the National Labor Relations Act in 1935 and the Fair Labor Standards Act in 1938. These two acts incorporated many of the provisions of the agreements contemplated by the states.

plan from national officials at the Governors' Conference in 1935, several of the state executives backed a resolution stating that the conference "does hereby protest against this policy and demands that full control of welfare relief administration be placed in the hands of the states. . . ." [5] The resolution failed to pass, and a more co-operative statement was substituted in its place, but the message was clear: the governors were in no mood to be left out of the plans for national recovery.

Of course, by no means all of the New Deal programs ignored the states or aggrandized the national government. It was during the New Deal that the phrase "co-operative federalism" was coined to describe the new—and generally amicable—partnership between Washington and the states as they jointly sought solutions to common problems. "Co-operative federalism" meant, first, that the national government had entered such areas as public welfare with national programs that would co-exist with state programs doing roughly the same thing. The state and national agencies "co-operated" in their attack on the substantive problem of welfare. Second, "co-operative federalism" implied a proliferation of federal grant-in-aid programs, in which the states and the national government relied on state agencies to perform the tasks but jointly shared the financing.

Large numbers of governors staunchly supported the extension of co-operative programs during the New Deal period. The attitude in bygone days had been that the national government should stay out of any matters touching on the sovereignty of the states. With prominent exceptions, the New Deal governors were more concerned

[5] *Proceedings,* 1935, pp. 105–106.

with the attack on problems of the depression than with the theoretical defense of states' rights. During the thirties the battle over the right of the national government to introduce new programs affecting the states was largely stilled. At the annual Governors' Conferences, for example, the state executives would fulminate and fuss about the manner in which the national government was acting, but from the beginning of the New Deal onward there was little expectation of a complete national withdrawal from areas previously controlled by the states. What the New Deal governors expected and sought, in the main, were modifications in federal procedures, not abolition of national programs.

One question immediately arises: did party affiliation have anything to do with the attitude of the governors toward the New Deal? There were more Republicans than Democrats in the governors' ranks during the twenties, but the Democrats controlled a healthy majority of the statehouses in the thirties. Did this mean, then, that the Democrats were behind Roosevelt and the Republican governors were against him? There was, strangely, very little correlation between party label and policy positions taken by the governors. Even during the height of the New Deal, each party had violent critics of Roosevelt represented in the conference. Some Republican governors had been elected in the thirties by "out-dealing" the New Deal Democrats and were strong Roosevelt supporters. Some Democratic governors were among the most unyielding opponents of the New Deal.

The overriding fact of the period was not that certain governors favored the New Deal while others opposed it, but rather that governors on both sides of the fence had accepted the clear necessity of being involved in national politics. The Governors' Conference in the thirties talked about national issues with gusto. They passed public resolutions on national questions with no regard for the moribund conference tradition against resolutions. And they began to look around for more workable means of putting their opinions into action.

The Birth of COSGO

Ever since the inception of the Governors' Conference, the governors had retained an executive secretary, but his work had been on a part-time basis which involved no more than making the arrangements for the annual meetings. The governors needed a permanent staff to execute their policies and to gather and analyze information. When they acquired such a staff, they entered a second stage in their transition to an activist organization.

Governors had occasionally suggested that the conference should have a professional secretariat, but no action had been taken. Yet developments elsewhere promised eventually to modify the thinking of the governors. Around the country, state legislators were also pressing for agencies of interstate co-operation. In 1930, with $20,000 support and a history of half-successes to its credit, the American Legislators' Association opened shop in Chicago under the leadership of State Senator Henry Toll, of Colorado. Other groups were also taking shape in Chicago: the Public Administration Clearing House; the American Municipal Association; the American Public Welfare Association; the Municipal Finance Officers' Association; and the Governmental Research Association.

On October 22, 1933, the leaders of the American Legislators' Association officially established the Council of State Governments—COSGO for short. Unlike the Governors' Conference or the American Legislators' Association, the council was an institution technically composed of state governments rather than of individuals. Its members were commissions on interstate co-operation created by the states. Its participants, as members of the interstate commissions, were state legislators, governors, and members of state executive departments.

Originally devoted primarily to the development of interstate compacts, the Council of State Governments soon acquired new duties as a service agency for different national organizations. In 1936 the council did research for the National Association of Attorneys General, the National Association of Secretaries of State, and the American Legislators' Association.

It is not surprising, then, that when the Governors' Conference got interested in creating a professional staff, they looked to the Council of State Governments for help. The governors secured the research services of the council on an informal basis in 1936, and the council executive director, Henry Toll, helped organize the 1937 and 1938 Governors' Conferences. Finally in 1938, when the governors needed a new secretary-treasurer, they chose the new director of the Council of State Governments, Frank Bane.

Frank Bane's dual role as director of the council and secretary to the governors was the buckle that joined the two institutions. What happened was not a merger—the organizations retained distinctly separate identities—but rather an interlocking of leadership whereby the governors gained the permanent staff services of the Council of State Governments without losing their own autonomy.[6]

If this study were devoted to interstate co-operation in general, rather than to the transformation of state governors as a particular body of leaders, attention would need to be centered on the Council of State Governments and its total program. There is a need for a good history of the council. There is also need for analyses of the work of other associations of state officials which draw upon the staff services of the council—the associations of budget officers, purchasing officers, legislators, and attorneys-general. Any comprehensive study of recent state government in the United States must take into account all of these groups.

Moreover, the work of the Governors' Conference from 1938 onward cannot be isolated from the activities of the Council of State Governments. When reference is made to a resolution passed by the conference, to a statement made before a congressional committee by the conference executive committee, or to a major study undertaken by the governors, the professional work of the council staff is usually visible behind the scenes. For purposes of this study, the role of the council must be restricted to its service to the Governors' Conference. At the same time it must be emphasized that this service represents only a portion of the work of the Council of State Governments.

[6] For further background on the formation of the Council of State Governments and its eventual alliance with the Governors' Conference, see Frank Bane, "The Governors' Conference and the Council of State Governments," *Proceedings*, 1938, xx-xxii; Henry W. Toll, "Four Chapters Concerning the Council of State Governments," *State Government*, Vol. XI (November, 1938), pp. 199–205; Henry W. Toll, "The Founding of the Council of State Governments," *State Government*, Vol. XXXII (Summer, 1959), pp. 162–64; and Frederick L. Zimmerman, "Fourteen Creative Years," *State Government*, Vol. XXXII (Summer, 1959), pp. 164–73.

Similarly, the emphasis in this study on national politics should not distort the fact that the Governors' Conference and the Council of State Governments make a gigantic day by day contribution to the solution of internal state problems. Working with the professional staff, the governors have attacked a myriad of technical state matters in recent years. The staff has prepared comprehensive studies of state public-school systems, state-supported higher education, mental health, metropolitan problems, highway safety and motor truck regulation, care of older citizens, occupational licensing legislation, and other equally important state problems.

Most important of all, the combined efforts of the conference and the council have helped to strengthen the financial and organizational structure of the American states: The Council of State Governments publishes annual volumes of suggested state legislation which are often used to reform state laws, and improvements have been fostered in administrative and legislative procedures. The strengthened position of many a governor can be attributed partly to the influence of the conference and the Council of State Governments. The publications and consultants of these organizations have incessantly advocated administrative reforms which would give the governors greater authority.

These internal improvements have been of exceptional importance for the stability of the states. One scholar believes that the greatest contribution of the Governors' Conference has been its work in transforming the internal quality of state government. Improvements, says Joseph Harris, "are due in part to the great expansion in the size, cost, and importance of state government, but the Gover-

nors' Conference has played an important part in the
transformation." [7] In the long run, the internal state improvements may also prove to be the greatest contribution
of the states toward the preservation of the federal system.
For without internally strong state government, the probability of increased national control becomes almost a
certainty.

The Challenge of War

The governors were organized. What, then, would they
do? War gave them a ready answer, for the Japanese attack
on Pearl Harbor rallied the governors together in the service of the nation. Their contribution to eventual victory
cannot be measured in terms of gold stars or Purple Hearts,
but their work was truly exceptional, and their ability to
unify the efforts of the states marked another stage in the
development of an effective national consciousness among
the governors.

Confronted with a task of civilian mobilization more
complicated than any conceived in the past, the national
government had to rely heavily on the chief executives of
the states for the administration of the civilian defense
effort. Working closely with the professional staff of the
Council of State Governments, the governors led their
states in the creation of state councils of defense throughout the nation. In co-operation with the Department of
Justice, governors attacked the problems of law enforcement in a wartime economy. Executive committees of the
conference labored over the revision of tax structures to

---

[7] Joseph P. Harris, "The Governors' Conference: Retrospect and Prospect,"
State Government, Vol. XXXI, (Summer, 1958), pp. 190–96, quoted at p. 193.

meet the national emergency. State administrations across
the country developed uniform regulations on such subjects as blackout precautions, public health and sanitation,
and federal defense grants. The administration of the Selective Service System by the states, under the leadership
of the governors, was the basis of the military recruitment
program.

The Japanese attack compounded the domestic crisis,
for the nation found itself faced with serious shortages of
essential commodities which could be controlled only
through a rigorous rationing program. Barely a week after
the Pearl Harbor strike, the Office of Price Administration, which had been given primary responsibility for
rationing, asked the governors to set up co-operative machinery in the states. Every governor responded favorably
and immediately undertook one of the memorable administrative feats in American history.

Drawing upon the existing resources of the states, the
governors and the OPA put into action a nationwide program of rationing in the space of three weeks. The first
rationed commodity was tires; then automobiles were
added, then sugar, and ultimately many more scarce commodities. Most impressive of all was the fact that virtually
every American family was registered for rationing in a
period of four afternoons in the public schools of the nation.[8]

A committee of the Governors' Conference, in co-opera-

[8] Interview with Frank Bane, July 13, 1959. During the war Mr. Bane
worked with OPA as well as with the Council of State Governments and
the Governors' Conference. For a more detailed account of the wartime ac
tivities of the states, see Frank Bane, "The Citizen Civilian Army," in Leonard
D. White, ed., *Civil Service in Wartime* (Chicago: University of Chicago
Press, 1945), pp. 142–59.

tion with the national Committee on Federal-State Co-operation in the War Effort, prepared uniform motor transport standards to insure efficient movement of the materials of war. The same group made plans for the famous 35-mile-an-hour speed limit which all states en-forced for the conservation of tires and gasoline.

During the war years the agenda of the Governors' Con-ference was dedicated almost exclusively to questions of national defense. Nearly every aspect of the defense effort was discussed—industrial production, selective service, agriculture, civilian defense, emergency war powers, ra-tioning and price control, and other related problems. The governors in the war years also brought national ad-ministrators and other leaders to their conferences for discussions about state co-operation in the defense effort.

In depression days any co-operation between governors and the national government was done solely on an indi-vidual basis. In distinct contrast, the governors' wartime effort was co-ordinated through the offices of the Gover-nors' Conference. Policies were developed within the con-ference and in the staff facilities of the Council of State Governments. These policies were picked up by the gov-ernors and put into effect in their home states. The confer-ence staff served as communications center for the gover-nors, and as a liaison center for work with the national government.

The Triumph of a Policy of Action

Although the governors were zealous in their support of the defense effort, they were also firm in their guardian-ship of functions which they felt belonged to the states. A number of these functions had been pre-empted by the national government in the name of national security, while other functions were threatened.

Until 1942, for example, the states handled the administration of all unemployment compensation. But early in 1942 Congress proposed to establish a special nationally-financed unemployment program for persons dislocated by the conversion to a war economy. The Governors' Conference executive committee quickly organized a formal protest before the House Ways and Means Committee, arguing that the proposal undermined the existing system of unemployment insurance and contributed nothing to the war effort.[9] Other interest groups joined the governors, and despite support for the bill from labor groups, the committee voted to table the bill and effectively thwarted action on the war-displacement project.

The governors backed up their determination to bargain with the national government in several ways. At their 1943 meeting the governors directed the conference executive committee to examine national laws and rules relating to peacetime activities and to propose amendments to federal statutes which would return administrative authority for peacetime government services to the states. After the governors had examined these proposed amendments, the executive committee would then "proceed to arrange to have amendments introduced in Congress, and work out lobby procedures to get them passed."[10]

At the same time, the conference staff expanded its

[9] U.S., Congress, House, Committee on Ways and Means, *War Displacement Benefits, Hearings on H.R. 6559*, 77 Cong., 2 sess., February 11–17, 1942
[10] *Proceedings*, 1943, p. 131.

Washington office to keep close watch over national activities affecting the states. Proposed bills which were deemed important to the states were sent to the interested parties for their examination. A legislative service was established to digest pending national legislation and administrative orders, and governors received copies of these digests.

What prompted this militant new attitude among the governors? There was a variety of motivations, but perhaps the most important was summarized by Turner Catledge, a correspondent for the *New York Times,* who attended the 1943 session of governors. "It is not Federal aid that the Governors resent," he observed. "They asked for it during the depression and likely will ask for it again. Nor is it Federal power, as such. It is the usurpation of State functions inherent in the whole Federal-aid process, particularized nowadays by the operations of increasing thousands of Federal agents in various States." [11] The central figure in the metamorphosis of the Governors' Conference, Secretary-Treasurer Frank Bane, saw the development of an activist attitude as an act of political realism by the governors. The change came about, in his view, because the governors were faced with a loss of power, both individually and collectively. To maintain the federal structure as they understood it, they were forced to abandon their individuality in favor of strong collective action.[12]

Matching the new policy of action were several modifications in the procedures and structure of the Governors' Conference. One of the governors' first moves was to strengthen conference leadership. Their executive com-

[11] *New York Times,* June 27, 1943.
[12] Interview with Frank Bane, July 13, 1959.

mittee originally consisted of only three members but had
been enlarged to five in 1924. Under the pressures of wartime, however, when the committee was forced to meet as
many as six times a year, the governors expanded the committee to nine members. This move gave the committee
more manpower and greater flexibility in its operation.

Increasingly, the chairmanship of the executive committee had become a position of considerable responsibility rather than an honorary post. But since conference
tradition dictated that the chairman should be chosen by
the executive committee rather than by the full assembly,
the governors desiring to further the candidacy of a particular governor had to do their politicking through the
executive committee and not with the conference as a
whole. In 1959, to make the chairman directly responsible
to the entire conference, the governors provided for his
direct election.

Originally the governors had banned all policy resolutions, but when the tradition collapsed in the New Deal
period, the governors for a time passed resolutions by simple majority vote. Yet after the mid-thirties the conference
developed an unwritten rule that required unanimous
consent for the passage of any resolution. More than one
resolution was killed by a solitary dissenter in the conference, and the governors realized that effective policy statements would require a modification of the unanimity rule.
After several years of debate, in 1954 the governors
amended their procedure to allow three-fourths of the governors of all states to adopt resolutions over the protests
of a minority. In 1959 the rules were revised again to provide for approval of resolutions by two-thirds of the members present.

Another important modification of the conference came with a revision of its program techniques. Traditionally, the conference had listened patiently to numerous prepared papers jammed closely together on a schedule. There was little time for serious informal discussion and interchange of views. In 1944, Governor Thomas E. Dewey, of New York, led a major and eventually successful revolt against the deadening effects of a predigested agenda. Expressing his deep conviction that the Governors' Conference should be an opportunity for intense interchange about the problems confronting the governors, he pleaded for a conference arranged to give governors a maximum of time for private, informal discussions. He expressed publicly what most of the governors knew privately, that formal papers read in public session were designed mainly for home consumption and not for a critical examination of issues.[13] Dewey's hopes for private exchanges were not realized—there were important factions within the conference who felt that all, or nearly all, sessions should be open to the public and the press—but the agenda of postwar meetings definitely turned away from rigid recitations and employed the round-table device with increasing frequency.

During the time the governors were building their organization, conference attendance followed an erratic course. As shown in Figure 1, attendance in the early years had been reasonably good, but dwindled to a low of eleven governors in 1938 before it rallied and climbed to its near-perfect level in the postwar years.

The low turnout in the thirties is somewhat out of line with the fact that the national interests and activities of the

[13] *Proceedings*, 1944, pp. 176–78.

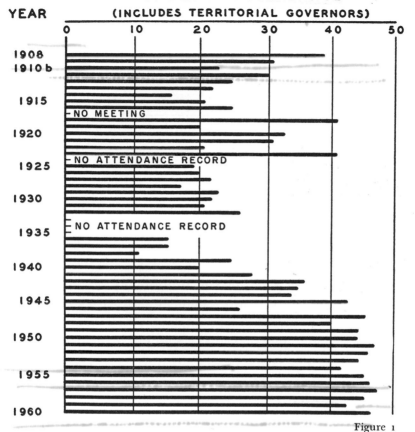

GOVERNORS' CONFERENCES
NUMBER IN ATTENDANCE
(INCLUDES TERRITORIAL GOVERNORS)

YEAR

1908
1910b

1915

—NO MEETING

1920

1925 —NO ATTENDANCE RECORD

1930

1935 —NO ATTENDANCE RECORD

1940

1945

1950

1955

1960

Figure 1

governors were reviving during the same period. Some
governors undoubtedly stayed away because they felt that
the conference had lost its efficacy. Others were detained
—as some nearly always are—by legislative sessions or political crises in their home states. In the thirties especially,
governors were absorbed in the economic crises of state
government.

On the other hand, the soaring attendance marks after World War II did not result entirely from the revitalized program of the Governors' Conference. The spread of fast and reliable air transportation probably accounted for increased attendance as much as any single factor. But whatever the reasons, the fact remains that contemporary governors do their utmost to be present at every annual conference.

Development of Regional Governors' Conferences

While the tendencies toward national uniformity directed the interests and activities of governors into national affairs, increasing sectional problems also generated organizations of governors in the geographical regions of the United States. Simultaneously, governors expanded their national and their regional activities. Although sporadic regional meetings of governors were held many times in earlier years, it was not until the New Deal era that regional associations became permanent political fixtures.

During the mid-thirties, southern state governors became deeply disturbed over what they regarded as discriminatory freight rates fixed by the Interstate Commerce Commission. They believed the South was treated unfairly in comparison to the East. A decision to take collective action to improve the southern rates was the basis for a conference of southern governors held in 1935. The first few meetings were indecisive, but by 1939 the Southern Governors' Conference had emerged as an effective organization with annual meetings.

After nearly ten years of litigation the governors scored

a partial success on freight rates when the ICC in 1952 handed down a decision favorable to the South. The southern governors also sought new defense industries for their region during the war. The conference was instrumental in the establishment of the Southern Regional Education Board in 1949, an interstate compact agency dedicated to the improvement of educational facilities in the area. More recently, the conference has dealt with such a complex problem as nuclear energy. At the 1956 Southern Governors' Conference, the governors advised the creation of nuclear energy advisory committees in each member state, and started a long-range program of regional development in nuclear energy.

The Southern Governors' Conference has been the most politically boisterous of the regional associations. Southern governors have not been regarded as strong presidential contenders because of their unacceptability in states outside the South, but this has never prevented them from being especially militant in their political comments during the annual conferences.

Tempers flared among the southern governors when the Roosevelt administration considered the abolition of the poll tax and the liberalization of labor and race relations policies. By 1948, the civil rights issue had become an item of major controversy at the annual southern conference. The governors undertook a general study of President Truman's civil rights policies in February, 1948. In March, a specially called meeting of the conference repudiated the leadership of Truman, foreshadowing the Dixiecrat rejection of the Democratic ticket in the November election.[14] When the Dixiecrats decided to offer their own candidates to the southern electorate, they chose Gover-

[14] *New York Times,* March 14, 1948.

nors J. Strom Thurmond, of South Carolina, and Fielding
L. Wright, of Mississippi, as presidential and vice-presi-
dential nominees. Both men were leaders in the Southern
Governors' Conference.

While the southern governors were fighting freight
rates and Yankee race policies, a group of New England
governors organized a similar regional association. To a
large degree the freight-rate activities of the southern governors prompted the New England governors to organize
in self-defense on freight-rate policies. The New Eng-
landers established an annual meeting and became forthright spokesmen of New England's interests. Borrowing
the idea of their southern colleagues, the New England
group also encouraged the creation in 1955 of a New England Board of Higher Education by means of a regional
interstate compact.

Perhaps the most vigorous regional association emerged
in the West. Drawn together by common interests in resource conservation, federal lands policy, water, power
development, and politics, the western state governors met
irregularly for a number of years and finally evolved a permanent organization. The western governors have issued
forthright policy resolutions on these subjects. They have
been active in Washington, where they have frequently
defended conference policies before congressional committees and executive agencies. In 1953, the Western
Interstate Commission for Higher Education was created
under the sponsorship of the Western Governors' Conference.

There is a steady communication between the regional
governors' associations and the national Governors' Conference. A regional group interested in a particular policy

issue may carry its problem to the national association in order to give it further consideration and publicity. Policy resolutions of the regional associations may closely parallel resolutions in the national conference. An example is found in the case of the federal-state highway program, in which both southern and western regional conferences passed resolutions similar to the national conference resolutions.

The New Dispensation

Generally, the revolution in the outlook of the governors was ignored by the public, the press, and scholars. The change was, understandably, a minor one in the context of the larger issues facing the nation. A change in outlook and approach, moreover, did not necessarily promise a change in results. The evolution of the governors' decision to engage actively in national policy-making did not guarantee effectiveness. Nevertheless, by the end of the war a few observers had noticed something different about the governors.

Thomas L. Stokes, Pulitzer Prize winning journalist and close observer of the Governors' Conference, felt in 1944 that the governors were coming back into their own. "After some groping," he said, "they seem to be finding their proper places of power, influence, and usefulness in a new dispensation of cooperative relationship with the federal government. . . ." [15] This relationship could be, he thought, the salvation of the federal system of American government. Recognizing that the failure of the states to

---

[15] Thomas L. Stokes, "The Governors," *State Government,* Vol. XVII (June, 1944), p. 343–46.

respond to urgent social needs was one of the prime causes of national action in many areas, Stokes did not believe that the old federal balance would be restored without alteration. Rather the "new dispensation" of co-operation between the national government and the states would be the standard of the future. The task of the governors, in his view, was to adjust the machinery of the states to operate most effectively within the new federal arrangement.

The next two chapters explore in detail the ways in which the modern Governors' Conference has concerned itself with national policies. Chapter 4 deals with the influence of the governors on Capitol Hill. Chapter 5 examines the relationship between the governors and the executive branch, with special attention to joint federal-state studies of intergovernmental relations.

4

The Governors and Congress

CONGRESS hums with the activity of so many lobby groups that it is always difficult to single out the role that the governors have in the enactment of national legislation. But there are instances—some of which are discussed as case studies in this chapter—when the concerted influence of the state governors is clearly evident. Especially since World War II, when the activist techniques of the Governors' Conference matured to a point of effectiveness, gubernatorial influence in Congress has grown until it is worthy of special notice.

A glance at the resolutions passed by the Governors' Conference in recent years reveals how the governors have become absorbed in congressional policy issues. Between 1943 and 1959, 60 per cent of all resolutions passed by the conference were addressed entirely or in part to the national government. Of these national policy resolutions, over two-thirds were aimed at Capitol Hill. In marked contrast, only 17 per cent of conference resolutions were directed to state governments.

The subjects of greatest concern to the governors during this period, judging from the contents of their resolutions, were national military and civil defense policy and general federal-state relations.[1] Often, the governors have backed up their resolutions with testimony before congressional committees. In a sixteen-year period after 1943, for example, 148 governors entered testimony before committees a total of 781 times. Sometimes the governors testified by letter but most frequently by personal appearance. On some occasions the governors appeared on their individual initiative, but in many instances the testimony was directly sponsored or indirectly prompted by the Governors' Conference. A peak of activity was reached in 1955, when governors formally expressed their views to congressional committees a total of 133 times during the year.

Case Studies of Action in Congress

Five case studies have been chosen to illustrate the methods used by the Governors' Conference to influence Congress and to show the varied and occasionally surprising stands which the governors have taken on matters of national policy. The selected policy studies include: employment security, federal aid to airport construction, public assistance, civil defense, and the interstate highway program. These cases have concerned the governors for a number of years and involve issues which will continue to appear on Governors' Conference agenda year after year.

---

[1] On many of these topics, Governors' Conference policy has been shaped in co-operation with other public and private interest groups. For example, the governors have passed resolutions on the National Guard in league with the National Guard Association and resolutions on highway safety in co-operation with the National Safety Council.

The Governors' Conference itself has been lobbied heavily by interest groups who seek the support of the governors. Representatives of business, labor, and public agencies are customarily present at modern Governors' Conferences to negotiate in private about conference resolutions.

As these cases will show, the governors have often fought for greater state autonomy but have also advocated, on several legislative issues, increased national participation or leadership in a co-operative federal-state venture. In some instances the governors have reversed their position in response to changing political conditions, moving from a traditional defense of state powers, in a particular issue, to an advocacy of greater national power.

Employment Security

Like most of the national policy issues which have interested the Governors' Conference, the federal-state unemployment insurance and employment service programs are complicated by many sub-issues and competing interests. The activities of the Governors' Conference cover only a part of the issues and pressures which make up the politics of employment security. Business and labor groups, along with national and state employment security officials, have maintained a continuing and intensive interest in nearly all phases of employment security, while the Governors' Conference has restricted its direct influence to a few key issues.

The federal-state employment security program has two major tasks: the operation of a nationwide system of unemployment insurance for persons who are out of work; and a related employment service which serves to put workers back into appropriate jobs as quickly as possible. Both phases of the program are administered principally by agencies of state government but are supervised and regulated under federal law.

Although some states had been at work on the employment security problem for many years,[2] the national government gave the program new life in the early days of the New Deal. The Wagner-Peyser Act of 1933, now amended in several details, is the basis for the operation of state employment services under the aegis, though not the direct control, of the Bureau of Employment Security in the Department of Labor.

The unemployment insurance phase of the program is grounded in the Federal Unemployment Tax Act and the Social Security Act of 1935. A 3 per cent federal tax was levied on the payrolls of employers, but the laws provided that the states could be credited with 90 per cent of this tax if they set up unemployment taxes of their own in conformity with federal regulations. This meant that only 10 per cent of the tax would go to the national government. State-collected tax money, not federal money, is paid to unemployed workers. The national government finances the administrative costs of the operation of the state employment services and unemployment compensation programs. Within these programs, the national government retains substantial power to oversee the performance of state agencies.[3]

World War II brought further changes in the federal-state employment security relationship. After the attack on Pearl Harbor, President Roosevelt issued an order bringing all state employment services under direct na-

[2] As early as 1890 Ohio had opened a free employment office.
[3] For a thorough review of the administrative and political background of employment security, see Francis E. Rourke, *Intergovernmental Relations in Employment Security*, Research Monograph No. 6, *Intergovernmental Relations in the United States as Observed in the State of Minnesota,* edited by William Anderson and Edward W. Weidner (Minneapolis: University of Minnesota Press, 1952). See especially Chapters One and Three. Also see U.S., Commission on Intergovernmental Relations, Vol. VII: *A Study Committee Report on Unemployment Compensation and Employment Service* (Washington: Government Printing Office, June, 1955).

tional control. In September, 1942, the services were placed under the jurisdiction of the War Manpower Commission. The logic of such a move was convincing: the enormous mobilization effort required highly centralized employment facilities. The temporary nature of the move was stressed, and governors acceded to the emergency measure.

The loss of the state employment services, however temporary, was nevertheless a threat to the existing balance of power between the states and the national government in the administration of employment security. There were apprehensions that the employment services might never be returned to the states after the war. Even more disturbing to some governors was the thought that the temporary loss of the employment services might signify an ultimate loss of the related unemployment compensation program. "Anxious as they undoubtedly were to contribute in every way possible to the successful prosecution of the war, a good many state administrators could not wholly rid themselves of the suspicion that something had been put over on them by the national agency under the guise of the war emergency." [4]

By the time of their annual meeting in 1944, the governors had grown publicly restive about the nationalization of the employment services. They resolved that "as soon as practicable" the employment services should be placed once again in the hands of the states. They further resolved that the executive committee should follow the situation, and if it appeared that the time had come when the services should be returned to the states, the committee was authorized to notify the president.[5]

[4] Francis E. Rourke, *op. cit.*, p. 37.
[5] *Proceedings*, 1944, pp. 194–95.

A year later the governors were even more disturbed about the situation. They resolved that the employment services should be returned to the states "as soon as effective arrangements for such transfer can be made." The conference instructed the executive committee to work for an immediate return to the original method of operation.[6]

In August, 1945, the conference executive committee met with President Truman to urge him to give back the employment services to the states. According to a report of conference chairman Edward Martin, Governor of Pennsylvania, the President agreed in principle that the employment services should be returned eventually but insisted that the national government should retain control for a while longer.[7] Initially, the President had stated that the employment services should stay under national jurisdiction until June 30, 1947.[8]

Temporarily defeated in their attempt to secure presidential support for an immediate transfer, the governors, along with other interested groups, turned their energies to Congress, where there was strong sentiment for the return of the employment agencies to the states. Governor Martin, representing the conference, appeared before the Senate Finance Committee to testify in late August, 1945.[9]

Although separate legislation had been introduced to

[6] *Ibid.*, 1945, p. 225.

[7] *Ibid.*, 1946, p. 10.

[8] *New York Times,* Jan. 6, 1946.

[9] U.S., Congress, Senate, Committee on Finance, *Hearings, Emergency Unemployment Compensation, S. 1274,* 79 Cong., 1 sess., August 29–September 4, 1945. The Governors' Conference testimony was also entered in U.S., Congress, House, Committee on Ways and Means, *Hearings, Unemployment Compensation Act of 1945, H.R. 3736,* 79 Cong., 1 sess., August 30–September 7, 1945.

effect the return of the services, pro-state strategists chose to attach a similar provision to a major appropriation bill, the President's own $51 billion Appropriation Rescission Bill, thereby making it even harder for the President to refuse to comply with the governors' demands.

The pro-state strategists had miscalculated the importance that President Truman attached to the Employment Service. After the appropriation bill had been through conference and both houses had approved the conference report, the President decided to pocket veto the entire bill solely on the grounds that it would require the divestment of national control over the employment agencies within one hundred days after the law went into effect. In his veto message of December 22, 1945, the President said, "While I believe such a transfer should be made at the proper time, I am convinced that this bill requires that it be made at the wrong time, and in the wrong way." [10] The President also stressed his original position that the services should remain under national control until June, 1947.

Starting again, after their defeat by President Truman, the governors renewed their efforts in the second session of the Seventy-ninth Congress when it convened in January, 1946. At a meeting of the executive committee on January 5, the governors planned their approach and instructed the chairman to arrange another face-to-face meeting with President Truman. The *New York Times* felt that "The [governors'] action made certain a bitter fight after Congress returns from its holiday recess to pass new legislation replacing the rider . . . which caused

[10] U.S., *Congressional Record,* 79 Cong., 1 sess., Vol. 91, 1946, part 9, p. 12547.

President Truman to veto on December 23 a $51,000,000,-
000 bill. . . ." [11]

In the new congressional session Congressman Everett
M. Dirksen supported the pro-state forces with a bill which
would require the return of the employment services
within thirty days after enactment. The hearings on employment service legislation at this juncture did not include a single governor. Arrayed in favor of immediate
return of the service were such groups as the Interstate
Conference of Employment Security Agencies; the State,
County and Municipal Workers of America (CIO); the
Chamber of Commerce; and the National Association of
Manufacturers. Against the immediate return of the service were various labor leaders, the director of the United
States Employment Service, the League of Women Voters,
and the NAACP.

Although the Dirksen bill, somewhat modified, passed
the House successfully, it bogged down in the Senate Education and Labor Committee. There followed a series
of confusing parliamentary tactics which finally produced
a rider attached to another appropriations bill—this time
the Labor-Federal Security Appropriation for 1947. With
differing versions offered by both houses of Congress, and
with the governors and other groups working hard in the
background, a conference committee worked out a compromise proposal for the return of the employment services to the states as of November 15, 1946. Finally, after
both houses had adopted the conference report, the bill
was approved on July 20, 1946, and four months later
the states resumed control.

The governors took most of the credit for the victory,

[11] *New York Times,* January 6, 1946.

in truth, a larger measure than they really deserved. Governor Millard F. Caldwell, of Florida, addressing the governors at their 1947 meeting in Salt Lake City, reported on the employment service episode:

> When reluctance developed in Washington to return of the employment service to the states, in accordance with previous agreement, the Governors' Conference and the Council of State Governments brought the position of the states forcefully to the attention of the President and the Congress. The employment offices were handed back to us . . . and generally, are functioning with greatly increased efficiency.[12]

Without pausing over this accomplishment, the governors pressed ahead with a second major task on the agenda of employment security—the revision of the method of handling the administrative costs of the employment security program. Under existing law, the national government apportioned money to the states for the operation of the employment security offices according to a calculation of their needs. But the total amount apportioned to the states, even when added in with the amount spent for the national portions of the program, was considerably less than the total revenue taken in by the national government from their share of the payroll tax. The remaining national balance was used for other purposes. To the governors, this meant that the national government was making off with several million dollars that rightfully belonged to the unemployment compensation program.

At their 1947 conference, the governors advocated that the federal payroll tax should be "substantially relin-

[12] *Proceedings*, 1947, p. 8.

quished" to the states. They added that adjustments should be made on behalf of the states which would lose money, if the states assumed complete authority.[13]

Seven years later, the Eighty-third Congress passed legislation which earmarked the federal share of the payroll tax for employment security purposes. Under the provisions of the act, after administrative expenses have been paid to the states and the national agencies, any balance that remains in the national government's share of the payroll tax is placed in a special account called the Unemployment Trust Fund. This fund can be used for loans to states whose benefit funds have been exhausted by payment of unemployment claims. Governors were not entirely responsible for the change, but their influence was substantial.

Airport Construction

The Federal Aid for Airports Act of 1946 was one of the most controversial items of federal-state legislation in the postwar decade and was the subject of concentrated efforts of the Governors' Conference. The principal controversy was not over the fact of federal assistance in the construction of airports—that practice had been well established, although in rather unsystematic form, for a number of years. The issue was whether the national government should deal directly with municipalities, or should negotiate entirely with the state governments acting on behalf of the municipalities.

Strong factions in the national government joined forces

[13] *Ibid.*, 1947, pp. 281–82.

with leaders of many cities to support the premise that the national government should deal directly with the cities. The Governors' Conference detected that this premise was a blow to state authority. They countered with the proposition that all federal aid for airports should be approved by state aviation authorities. The final settlement of the controversy required months of debate in a congressional conference committee and represented a compromise between the conflicting points of view.[14]

Action on federal aid to airports began in 1945 with the introduction of two bills in the Senate, to provide federal assistance for development, construction, improvement, and repair of public airports. Neither bill contained a provision requiring the national government to channel its business through state agencies rather than to deal directly with individual municipalities.

The Governors' Conference executive committee mobilized a strong protest against the omission of the channeling requirement. In Senate hearings on the bills in March, 1945, members of the executive committee appeared to present their arguments.[15] In supporting the proposition that the program should be channeled through state government, the executive committee was backed by telegrams from forty-four governors who vigorously protested any legislation permitting direct federal-municipal negotiations. No governor took a contrary stand, and only

[14] For a comprehensive statement of the federal aid to airports program, see U.S., Commission on Intergovernmental Relations, Vol. XIII: *A Staff Report on Federal Aid to Airports* (Washington: Government Printing Office, June, 1955).

[15] U.S., Congress, Senate, Committee on Commerce, Subcommittee, *Hearings, Federal Aid for Public Airports*, 79 Cong., 1 sess., March 13–23, 1945. The governors' testimony begins on p. 314.

one, Ellis Arnall, of Georgia, replied that he had not had time to study the legislation and was unable to comment in time for the hearings.

In July, 1945, the annual meeting of the governors gave added weight to their defense of state authority by resolving that the Congress in its deliberations should follow "the long-established and effectively operated pattern of channelling aid to local communities exclusively through the respective state governments. . . ." [16] The governors pointed out that the concept of direct grants to political subdivisions of the states was "an entirely new method" which went against the tradition of federal-state co-operation. They contended that the new method would duplicate existing state organizations and would require a massive expansion of national facilities without proper need.

When the bills went to the Senate floor in modified form, Senator Ralph Owen Brewster, of Maine, formerly a chairman of the Governors' Conference executive committee, led a successful fight to amend the legislation to require all federal funds to be channeled through state government. According to Frank Bane, who was then Secretary-Treasurer of the Governors' Conference, the amendment was inspired by the governors and their staff at the Council of State Governments. [17]

The victory in the Senate was short-lived, for the House of Representatives passed their own version of the airport construction act which omitted the channeling requirement sponsored by Senator Brewster. The competing versions of the bill were sent to a conference commit-

[16] *Proceedings*, 1945, p. 224.
[17] Interview, July 13, 1959.

tee. Conferees were deadlocked for months over the issue
of channeling funds through the states, with the Republicans supporting the states' position and the Democrats
generally supporting the direct federal-municipal plan.
When the deadlock was finally broken, the channeling requirement was omitted from the conference report.

On the Senate floor the conference report was attacked
by supporters of the Governors' Conference, notably Senator Brewster and another former chairman of the conference executive committee, Senator Leverett Saltonstall, of Massachusetts. But the power of the governors'
supporters was insufficient to carry the day. The channeling requirement was not reinstated in the bill. Instead, a compromise provision which gave partial succor
to the governors was included in the final version of the
bill. The act did not require municipalities to channel
their requests through the states but permitted the states
to pass their own laws requiring municipalities to submit
all requests through a state agency. The states could compel channeling only if they could muster sufficient votes
in their own legislatures to make the requirement a matter of state law. This provision was quite different from
the objectives of the governors, who wanted the national
government to make the channeling mandatory.

Taking note of the fact that the national government
had thrown responsibility for mandatory channeling back
in the laps of the states, the governors at their 1946 meeting registered their disapproval of the legislation. They
repeated their support for an airport aid program operated "in accordance with the long-established, success-
fully-operated pattern of federal-state cooperation," that
is, a program in which federal law made the states the

prime factors in dealing with the national government. The governors also urged the states to develop aviation authorities and to enact legislation requiring municipalities to clear all airport aid requests through state agencies.[18]

The states were slow to enact channeling laws. By the time of the 1947 Governors' Conference, only about half of the states had required that federal grants be channeled through state aviation agencies. Once again the governors turned to the national government for assistance in creating the uniformity which the states themselves seemed unable to establish. They asked the Congress to enact legislation similar to their original bill, but Congress did not take action on their request.[19]

A year later, the governors made another effort to secure the passage of federal legislation to replace the inadequate work of the state legislatures, which by 1948 had passed compulsory channeling laws in only slightly more than half the states. The force of the states was rapidly being spent; national action to require channeling was the only plausible alternative. Congress again ignored the requests of the governors, however, and the basic channeling procedures of the airports act remained unchanged. After 1948 the governors lost interest and turned to other national issues.

Public Assistance

The politically delicate arena of public assistance has been entered by the governors at several points and with

[18] *Proceedings*, 1946, pp. 199–200.
[19] *Ibid.*, 1947, pp. 279–80.

varying degrees of success. Usually the governors have acted as defenders of state authority in the federal-state public assistance program. However at times they have placed their main emphasis on the co-operative solution of a substantive problem, such as the lack of uniformity in state residence requirements for public assistance eligibility.

The federal-state public assistance program is rooted in the Social Security Act and presently consists of four major categories of public assistance, financed jointly by the states and the national government on a matching-funds basis: Old-Age Assistance, Aid to the Blind, Aid to Dependent Children, and Aid to the Permanently and Totally Disabled. Conflicts between the states and the national government have arisen over substantive issues in the program as well as procedural matters involving the authority of the states.

One of the best illustrations of gubernatorial action in public assistance concerned a dispute between the governors and the national government over the disclosure of public assistance rolls. An amendment to the Social Security Act in 1939 stipulated that no states could publish the names of persons on public assistance rolls. There had been abuses by political candidates who used the rolls for campaign purposes. Under the 1939 amendment, any state which published the rolls would be subject to withdrawal of federal funds. Those who favored the secrecy rule—and officials in the Federal Security Agency were among its firm advocates—believed that the secrecy was necessary to prevent further political abuses. They also believed that individuals on the assistance rolls would be embarrassed by the publication of their names. Opponents of the secrecy rule—including most governors—believed that the publication of names was an essential part of weeding out cheaters and freeloaders who did not deserve to be on the assistance rolls. They believed that the only way to prevent political abuses was for the states to safeguard the use of public assistance rolls rather than to prohibit their publication altogether.

Underlying the arguments of the opponents of the secrecy rule was a general hostility toward the coercive tactics of the social security officials in Washington. Many governors had found themselves confronted by ultimatums from the national government concerning phases of the state public assistance program. Even more rankling to some governors were the rebuffs by their own state-employed public assistance personnel whose loyalties (conveniently insulated by civil service protection) were directed more toward the national government than the state which employed them.

Indiana reached a showdown with the national government over the no-disclosure rule in 1951. The Indiana legislature legalized publication of public assistance rolls, and on July 31, 1951, the Federal Security Administrator cut off Indiana's federal assistance funds. The state promptly carried its case into federal district court, which supported the Federal Security Administrator. Meanwhile, Indiana's Senator Jenner had been trying to get an amendment through Congress which would legalize the publication of public assistance rolls. After a successful move in the Senate, the amendment was thrown out by a conference committee on July 11. More influence was needed from some quarter.

The Governors' Conference of 1951 met at Gatlinburg, Tennessee, on September 30. On the third day of their meeting, Governor Thomas E. Dewey presided over a round-table discussion of social security problems. His guests were Federal Security Administrator Oscar R. Ewing and Social Security Commissioner Arthur J. Altmeyer. With these national officials in an open line of fire, the governors leveled a barrage against the practices of the public assistance program, and in particular against the no-disclosure rule. Governor James F. Byrnes proposed, in the presence of the national officials, that the conference should pass a resolution urging Congress to give the states full discretion in the publication of public assistance rolls. Governor G. Mennen Williams pointed out that the right of the states to publish the rolls did not mean that the states would necessarily authorize their publication. When Governor Dewey called for an expression of the governors' sympathies, there was unanimous support for the state position. Later, the conference adopted a formal resolution which read:

> The Governors' Conference has taken no position on the advisability or propriety of publicizing welfare rolls. The Governors' Conference is, however, unanimous in declaring that the publicizing of welfare rolls is a matter for determination by the individual states.[20]

Shortly after the governors expressed their views on the matter, the Congress accepted Senator Jenner's amendment to a revenue act giving the states the right to publish their assistance rolls.[21] A distinguished scholar took note of the action of Congress in this manner:

---

[20] *Ibid.*, 1951, p. 170.

[21] Public Law 183, Sec. 618, 65 Stat. 569 (1951). The law specified, however, that in order to qualify for federal assistance grants, states allowing publication must prohibit "the use of any list or names obtained through such access to such records for commercial or political purposes."

The quick response of Congress was obviously not due entirely to the attitude of the governors, but there can be no doubt that it carried weight in Congress. This incident suggests that the collective political power of governors (which is rarely put in motion) might carry considerable weight in refashioning future federal-state relations, insofar as governors find themselves in substantial agreement.[22]

The field of public assistance also affords an illustration of the systematic approach to national problems by the Governors' Conference. At their 1958 meeting the governors instructed the chairman to appoint a special committee of governors to study the problem of "stateless" persons—those who had recently moved from one state to another and because of residence requirements in their new state were ineligible for public assistance. The states had previously been criticized severely for their failure to make adequate provision for these stateless persons. Using background materials prepared by the conference staff at the Council of State Governments, the interim committee of the conference prepared a draft report for submission to the 1959 meeting of governors.

At their San Juan meeting, the governors devoted an entire afternoon to problems of public welfare and relief. The committee report was received with great interest and extensive discussion. Its importance was amplified by the presence of Arthur S. Flemming, Secretary of Health, Education, and Welfare. Later, the substance of the report was embodied in a conference resolution calling for Congress to establish a uniform one-year residence ceiling (permitting states, if they wished, to give even lower requirements) on the four federally-aided categories of

[22] Leonard D. White, *The States and the Nation* (Baton Rouge: Louisiana State University Press, 1953), p. 38.

public assistance, and encouraging state legislatures to ratify a contemplated interstate compact providing for aid to persons who had not qualified for residence requirements.

The notable feature of the governors' action on residence requirements was the studious and comprehensive manner in which they approached their problem. The ingredients were: a study by an interim committee; an extensive report to the conference; frank discussion in the presence of ranking national officials; and a resolution which would be used as a basis for further action by the Governors' Conference executive committee, staff members, and individual governors in their dealings with Congress and with state legislatures. It remains to be seen whether the governors' systematic work will produce concrete changes in the long-standing problem of stateless persons.

Civil Defense

The significance of civil defense in an age of nuclear weapons was carefully noted by the governors in the post-war years. Almost without exception they were outspoken advocates of improved civil defense techniques at a time when public apathy made civil defense one of the most neglected aspects of the over-all American security program. Three former governors—Millard F. Caldwell, of Florida; Val Peterson, of Nebraska; and Leo Hoegh, of Iowa—have served as national administrators of the civil defense effort. Individual governors have maintained close liaison with Washington in the development of effective state civil defense programs.

One fact should be stressed about the role of the governors in the formation of federal civil defense legislation: in this instance the governors initially favored state primacy in the civil defense effort but later shifted their position to favor national leadership and increased federal financial support. As this case will show, the governors have not always acted the part of defenders of state authority regardless of the program involved. On the contrary, the modern governors have been discerning in their attitudes toward federal programs. While they have often defended the authority of the states, they have also been willing to relinquish state primacy in areas where uniform national direction was a clear necessity, and particularly if federal funds promised to ease the financial burdens of the states.

In 1948, before a peacetime civil defense effort had been established, the Governors' Conference was generally agreed on two points: that a major civil defense effort was needed, and that the states should be the prime factors in the program. Governor J. Strom Thurmond, of South Carolina, caught the mood of the governors during a discussion of civil defense at their 1948 meeting. The states, he said, "must begin at once to accept their responsibility in the program, for civil defense is, after all, a state matter." At that time, the only federal agency was the Office of Civil Defense Planning, a forerunner of the Federal Civil Defense Administration. The planning agency in Washington, Thurmond noted, "is merely a coordinating agency designed to assist the states in carrying out the program." [23]

Working from the premise that the states should have

[23] *Proceedings*, 1948, p. 133.

primary responsibility in civil defense, the Governors' Conference asked its staff and executive committee to work with national officials in the development of federal legislation. They supported an effective national civil defense program but emphasized that "efficient operation cannot be achieved unless the federal government will work with and through the state governments." [24]

The governors' hopes for a state-centered civil defense plan were fulfilled in the comprehensive civil defense bill of 1950. The Federal Civil Defense Act of 1950 asserted that the responsibility for civil defense "shall be vested primarily in the several States and their political subdivisions. The Federal Government shall provide necessary coordination and guidance." [25] The act severely restricted the administrative and financial role of the national government. No federal money could be used for administrative or personnel expenses of the states, or procurement of land. The act allowed federal money to be used only on a matching basis for construction, leasing, and procurement of materials. The states were supposed to assume most of the responsibility for a sound civil defense program.

After a year of operating under the 1950 act, the governors had some sober second thoughts about a states' rights version of civil defense. The states were praised for their efforts in enacting civil defense legislation and in ratifying interstate compacts in civil defense activities, but the 1951 conference called upon the national government to step into civil defense more actively—most specifically by appropriating more funds. [26] At this stage of the civil defense

[24] *Ibid.*, p. 173.
[25] Public Law 920, 64 Stat. 1245 (1951).
[26] *Proceedings*, 1951, p. 168.

effort the recommendations were vague and ineffective. There followed a four-year period in which the Governors' Conference was silent on the subject.

In the meantime, American civil defense was slumping into a serious condition. State expenditures for civil defense were over $40 million in fiscal 1952; in fiscal 1953 they dropped to around $19 million; by 1954 they had plummeted to slightly over $8 million. In the four-year span between 1951 and 1955, the national government spent over $241 million, while the states spent roughly one-third that amount.[27] Yet the states were assigned by law the primary responsibility for the program.

Beginning in 1955 there was a major impulse to bring the civil defense program back to life. One strong voice of reform came from the Commission on Intergovernmental Relations, which recommended that the national government should assume primary responsibility, with the states and their subdivisions assuming a supporting role. The commission also favored direct relations between the national government and cities designated as critical target areas.[28]

Another move for reform came in the Congress. A subcommittee on civil defense of the Committee on Armed Services held hearings on the civil defense program in the spring and summer of 1955, while the House Committee on Government Operations held similar hearings a year

[27] U.S., Commission on Intergovernmental Relations, Vol. XII: *A Staff Report on Civil Defense and Urban Vulnerability* (Washington: Government Printing Office, June, 1955), p. 14.

[28] U.S., Commission on Intergovernmental Relations, Vol. I: *Report* (Washington: Government Printing Office, June, 1955), pp. 180–85. The Commission's recommendations were even more nationally oriented than those of its staff report, which had recommended a joint federal-state responsibility.

later.[29] At these hearings, Governors G .Mennen Williams, of Michigan; Christian A. Herter, of Massachusetts; and Averell Harriman, of New York, testified in favor of increased national responsibility for civil defense.

The 1955 Conference of Governors was also in a mood to work for fundamental changes in the civil defense program. They passed a resolution which recognized that the development of the H-Bomb, the dangers of nuclear fall-out, and other atomic dangers made civil defense "a national problem of tremendous magnitude" requiring sweeping revisions in existing civil defense legislation.[30]

Another step was the creation of a special committee on civil defense under the chairmanship of Governor Averell Harriman to consult with the national government and to report to the governors. The special committee entered into a protracted study of the civil defense problem, conferring with national officials and reporting to the conferences of 1956 and 1957.

It was not until 1958, however, that changes were made in the civil defense law. In July of 1957 the House Armed Services Committee reported a bill—H.R. 7576, called the Durham bill—designed to give the national government and the states joint responsibility in civil defense programs. The House passed the bill promptly and referred it to the Senate, where it faltered. Months went by, and when the Governors' Conference of 1958 assembled in May, the Senate Armed Services Committee had not yet reported the bill to the floor.

[29] U.S., Congress, Senate, Committee on Armed Services, Subcommittee on Civil Defense, *Hearings, Civil Defense Program*, 84 Cong., 1 sess., March 9–June 20, 1955; U.S., Congress, House, Committee on Government Operations, *Hearings, Civil Defense for National Survival*, 84 Cong., 2 sess., May 4–June 27, 1956.

[30] *Proceedings*, 1955, p. 141.

In an attempt to dislodge the bill from the Senate committee and secure its passage, the Governors' Conference issued a resolution that the Durham Bill be enacted by the Congress—thus endorsing the recommendation of the Governors' Conference special civil defense committee. Because the governors did not feel that the bill's provision for joint federal-state responsibility was adequate, they endorsed it with the comment that "While we believe that it does not go far enough toward recognition of the federal government's primary responsibility, its enactment would constitute a major step in the right direction." [31]

The governors' support of the Durham bill contributed to the fact that it was reported—with amendments—by the Senate Armed Services Committee on July 11, passed by the Senate on July 23, and signed into law on August 8, 1958. The act specified that it was the intention of Congress to vest responsibility for civil defense jointly in the national government and in the states and their subdivisions. The national government was given new authority to support the state programs in many categories rather than in just a few areas and was given important new authority in its own right.

The passage of the civil defense reform bill was the most important development in civil defense in recent years. Still the governors were not content to let matters lie at rest. The governors' committee on civil defense—whose chairmanship was assigned to Governor Nelson Rockefeller, of New York, after Governor Harriman went out of office—remained one of the most active committees of the Governors' Conference and communicated frequently with congressional committees, the president, and

[31] *Ibid.*, 1958, p. 167.

other officials in the executive branch. Governor Rockefeller evidenced a particular interest in protection from
radioactive fall-out, and much of the work of the special
committee was occupied with fall-out problems.

More and more the Governors' Conference was in-
clined to delegate interim authority to the civil defense
committee, which conducted studies of its own and passed
its own resolutions for submission to Senate and House
committees dealing with civil defense. The complexity
of civil defense legislation was certainly a justification for
the decentralization of authority to the committee. Decentralization was also symptomatic of the growing institutional stability of the Governors' Conference. The actions of the conference were taken with seriousness,
thoroughness, and with the definite intention of produc-
ing results. Resolutions had come to mean business—they
were not sonorous platitudes—and the interim work of
committees of the conference indicated the desire of the
conference to follow words with deeds.

Highway Construction

Governors have been perennially concerned with federal-state roads policy, from the first congressional appropriation for experimental post-road construction in
1912 to the revolutionary Federal-Aid Highway Act of
1956.[32] It was over the act of 1956, however, that the Governors' Conference made one of its most strenuous efforts
to influence the course of national legislation. Since the

[32] A good summary of federal highway legislation may be found in U.S.,
Department of Commerce, Bureau of Public Roads, *The Administration of
Federal Aid for Highways and Other Activities of the Bureau of Public
Roads*, Washington, January, 1957.

passage of the 1956 act, the governors have watched the development of supplemental legislation with careful eyes.

As in the case of civil defense legislation, the governors radically changed their position concerning the role of the national government in highway legislation. Initially they sought state primacy in financing and construction of highways of all kinds—primary, secondary, and interstate. But when they were confronted with the political facts about the interstate phase of the program, they abandoned their defense of state prerogatives in favor of a federally directed and financed interstate system. Nor did they merely acquiesce passively in the face of national leadership—they actively supported it.

At their 1952 session in Houston, the governors strongly favored a drastic transfer of taxing authority from the national government to the states, especially in the area of taxes applicable to highway construction. The most important tax was the federal gasoline tax, which then stood at two cents per gallon. The conference unanimously agreed that the national government should abandon the gasoline tax—implicitly giving the states free reign to enact state taxes to replace it—"as soon as may be consistent with needs of national defense," which then referred to the Korean emergency.[33] The governors were at this time anxious to win new powers for state government. They were also disturbed by the fact that the national government was distributing to the states only about two-thirds of the amount it collected in the gasoline tax. The remainder went for other federal expenditures.

The national government paid little attention to their entreaties. Instead, the Congress, in 1954, passed the larg-

[33] *Proceedings*, 1952, p. 195.

est federal-aid highway act in history, which authorized $2 billion for highway construction and included a $175 million initial appropriation for the massive interstate highway system.

At their 1954 meeting at Lake George, New York, some of the governors were taken aback by the action of the national government. Early in the meeting Governor James F. Byrnes, of South Carolina, remarked that he was "quite surprised a few months ago to read that the Congress had passed—and the President had signed—a bill increasing the appropriation for highways, at a time when the Governors seemed to be in accord that the grants should be reduced." Governor William Stratton, of Illinois, was annoyed at his colleagues for their lack of decisive action in influencing Congress, while Governor Robert B. Crosby, of Nebraska, urged the Governors' Conference to "double and triple and quadruple its efforts in the next Congress" to get the federal money returned to the states.[34]

The next development in the 1954 meeting almost completely reversed the thinking of the governors. President Eisenhower was scheduled to address the governors but was unable to attend because of the death of a member of his family. In his place he sent Vice-President Richard Nixon, who brought the President's prepared speech for delivery. The President, speaking through Mr. Nixon, launched a major new legislative proposal before the governors: "A $50 billion highway program in ten years," he said, "is a goal toward which we can—and we should—work."[35] The exact manner of financing the program was left unclear. It was not certain whether the President

[34] Ibid., 1954, pp. 31–41.
[35] Ibid., p. 90.

intended to increase federal participation or to invigorate state expenditures for highways. But the figure of $50 billion over a period of ten years stirred the thinking of every governor present.

It was obvious from discussion in the record on the following day that the sturdy principles of states' primacy had been visibly shaken by the proposal. The only decisive statement that could be mustered by the conference was a request to the Council of State Governments to cooperate on a study of the entire highway problem for consideration by the conference and eventual submission to the national government.

Working principally through a special highway committee under the chairmanship of Governor Walter J. Kohler, of Wisconsin, the governors gradually came to grips with the magnitude of the highway plan, and in so doing virtually reversed their field to favor national leadership and national financing. They even dropped their cardinal rule that the national government should abandon the gasoline tax. There were many crucial issues involved in the legislation—one of the principal disputes was whether it was to be financed on a pay-as-you-go basis or through deficit financing—but the arguments for state primacy in the new highway program lost most of their impetus. There was widespread acceptance of the principle that the national government would have to stand most of the costs of the interstate network.

The special committee of governors appeared before congressional committees several times when the President's bill was first proposed in 1955.[36] Congress failed to

[36] U.S., Congress, House, Committee on Public Works, *Hearings, National Highway Program, H.R. 4260,* 84 Cong., 1 sess., Part 1, April 18–June 1, 1955;

take any action in 1955, although the bill supported by the Governors' Conference came rather close to passage in the final days of the 1955 session.

The highway program was renewed in Congress in 1956 and emerged as Public Law 627, the most important highway legislation ever passed by the national government. In addition to legislation pertaining to primary, secondary, and federal roads, the bill authorized billions of dollars for construction and improvement of the interstate highway system, with 90% of the interstate costs to be borne by the national government. Moreover, the act increased the federal gasoline tax from two to three cents and substantially revised other taxes related to highway use.

The governors supported the major provisions of the bill, including the increase in the federal gasoline tax which they had originally sought to abolish. What caused this about-face by the governors? Admittedly some of the staunchest advocates of states' primacy had retired from office before the governors supported the increased federal role in highway construction, but many of the old-guard governors changed their position as well.

One conservative former governor, who was a key member of the special governors' highway committee, explained the reversal in an interview. Congress, he noted, was under heavy pressure to enact the highway bill with federal financing. The governors knew that the national government would not, indeed could not, get out of the gasoline tax field without wrecking the highway program.

U.S., Congress, Senate, Committee on Public Works, Subcommittee, *Hearings, National Highway Program, S. 1048, S. 1072, S. 1160, and S. 1573,* 84 Cong., 1 sess., February 21–April 15, 1955.

State legislatures were not strong enough to withstand
the pressures that would be exerted by the oil and gas
interests to cut the gasoline tax if the national government withdrew. In other words, all parties concerned—
the president, the Congress, and the governors, knew that
the national government was the only government politically and financially capable of levying the necessary
taxes for the highway program. Frank Bane, the Governors' Conference Secretary-Treasurer, when asked why
the governors decided to support national leadership,
smiled knowingly and quoted James Russell Lowell:

> New occasions teach new duties;
> Time makes ancient good uncouth;
> They must upward still, and onward
> Who would keep abreast of Truth.

Most of the provisions supported by the governors were
included in the legislation, but it must be remembered
that the highway bill was one of the most intensely lobbied
bills in congressional history. Many of the governors felt
that they were the principal figures. As former Governor
J. Howard Pyle, of Arizona, remarked in an interview:
"The governors were the voice of the people in this case.
No other groups had similar influence. It was the governors who drove the bargain." [37] Yet national officials, who
saw the legislation from the other side, assign less significance to the part of the governors. At best, the governors
were one appreciable force among many powerful forces.

After the passage of the basic interstate highway act,
the Governors' Conference kept an eagle eye on the progress of the program. Whenever the program lagged, the

[37] Interview, August 2, 1959.

conference passed resolutions calling for greater action, while the conference committee on roads and highway safety worked diligently with congressional and executive officials to keep the interstate program on the move.

Overview of the Cases

The five illustrations of Governors' Conference activity in Congress—employment security, airport construction, public assistance, civil defense, and highway construction—are cases in which the governors performed with a rather high degree of effort. In many other cases the interests of the governors extend no further than the simple expression of opinion through conference resolutions. Several observations can be made about the policy issues discussed here.

All of the cases suggest that the Governors' Conference accepted, almost unanimously, a permanent national interest in the fortunes of state government. While strong voices were raised in protest against the nature of national activities, there was a notable absence of fundamental protest against the basic concept of national participation in co-operative enterprises with the states.

The airport construction case indicates, moreover, that in some instances the governors have asked the national government to coerce them into doing certain things which they were unable to do themselves. Even when the national government made provision that any state could compel its cities to channel federal airport aid requests through state agencies, the governors continued to ask the Congress to pass a uniform national law requiring cities to channel their requests through the states—a tacit admission of political weakness of the states on this particular issue.

The efforts of the governors to secure the return of the employment services to the states; their defense of channeling provisions in the airport construction program; and their fight to win authority to publish public assistance rolls were all instances in which the governors acted as defenders of state authority and in which they achieved their goals with varying degrees of success. In this role, surely, the governors performed their traditional function. If the governors did not act as the watchdogs of state authority in the federal system, there is little likelihood that any other body of influential officials would do the same job with equal effectiveness. It is likely that many cases in the future will call upon the governors to gird themselves against what they regard as federal encroachments.

The role of the governors, in the cases presented here, did not stop with the defense of state authority. In their actions on public assistance residence requirements the governors worked toward a single federal law—not uniform state laws. In civil defense and the interstate highway system legislation the governors went even further, seeking additional national leadership and financial assistance in areas where they had originally demanded state primacy. Under the pressures of changing fiscal and political conditions, the governors gave up state authority in order to save the substance of important national programs.

The five cases also illustrate the increasing ability of the Governors' Conference to approach policy issues with systematic and sustained effort: using interim study committees, staff support, and carefully planned communication with Congress. The number of continuing Governors' Conference study committees increased from zero in 1945 to six in 1960. The committees have been continued from year to year in much the same manner as standing committees of the Congress. While the governors immediately after World War II were concerned with several policies at once, they made a determined effort on only two—employment security and airport construction. In contrast, the Governors' Conference of 1959 made sustained efforts to influence congressional action on highway funds, public assistance, taxation of state and local bonds, the National Guard, civil defense, and general intergovernmental relations. In each of these areas the governors assigned special committees or the executive committee to follow through on the policy stands taken by the governors. In addition, the 1959 conference expressed itself on other national issues without providing machinery for following through on the policies. This is approximately a reversal of the situation in 1945, when the governors expressed themselves on a number of issues but devised machinery to make their influence felt in only two areas.

The Governors' Bloc

The governors would have been much less effective in influencing Congress without inside help, much of which has come from the former governors who hold seats in the United States Senate. Jokingly called "The Governors' Bloc" by members of the press, the ex-governors in-the Senate are not a unified body but they nevertheless share many of the sympathies of the men who are serving as state governors, and their numbers are sufficient to pose a formidable threat in Senate strategy and voting. In the Eighty-seventh Congress of 1961–63 there were eighteen former governors; in times past there were even more.[38]

The former governors in the Senate have helped the Governors' Conference in several ways. They have encouraged conference representatives to appear in congressional hearings on behalf of special legislation. Members of the Senate Governors' Bloc have often sponsored legislation advocated by the Governors' Conference. In the Senate floor debate over the Federal Aid for Airports Act of 1946, leaders for the Governors' Conference position were Senators Ralph Owen Brewster and Leverett Saltonstall, both former chairmen of the Governors' Conference executive committee.

Finally, the Governors' Bloc in the Senate has been a reliable source of votes for bills sponsored by the Governors' Conference. In maneuvers over the airport construction act, for example, a crucial Senate vote concerned the mandatory channeling requirement favored by the conference. It was approved in the Senate forty to thirty-three but later deleted by the House. In an analysis of the Senate vote, Professor Morton Grodzins has observed that:

> The crucial factor bringing victory to the states was not party affiliation. It was the conduct of senators who had

[38] The former governors in the Senate in 1961 were: George D. Aiken, Vermont; J. Caleb Boggs, Delaware; H. Styles Bridges, N.H.; Harry F. Byrd, Va.; Frank Carlson, Kans.; Ernest Gruening, Alaska; Bourke B. Hickenlooper, Iowa; Spessard L. Holland, Fla.; Olin D. Johnston, S.C.; Robert S. Kerr, Okla.; Frank J. Lausche, Ohio; Edmund S. Muskie, Me.; John O. Pastore, R.I.; Richard B. Russell, Ga.; Leverett Saltonstall, Mass.; Andrew F. Schoeppel, Kans.; Herman E. Talmadge, Ga.; and J. Strom Thurmond, S.C.

once served as state governors. Sixteen ex-governors voted. Twelve were in favor of the amendment. Party identification made little difference: 5 of 6 Republican ex-governors and 7 of 10 Democratic ones supported the channeling amendment. Whereas 52 per cent of the senators who were not ex-governors opposed the amendment, 75 per cent of the ex-governors approved it. If the ex-governors had divided their votes in the same way as their fellow senators did, the amendment would have been defeated by one vote rather than winning by seven.[39]

[39] Morton Grodzins, "American Political Parties and the American System," unpublished mss., mimeo., p. 7., c. 1959.

5

The Governors and the President

RELATIONS between the governors and the White House have been erratic and sometimes discordant, but the record is rather clear on one central matter: in their dealings with the president, as with Congress, the governors have often encouraged the national government to preserve or expand its programs, even, on occasion, at the expense of state power. While the governors have been prompt to argue with presidents over programs which they felt belonged to the states, they have also urged presidents to keep other responsibilities off the shoulders of the states.

In Congress, the governors have attempted to influence national policy primarily through formal proceedings—the use of resolutions and testimony before congressional committees. In the executive branch, the influence has been more subtle and personal, but it has nevertheless created a steady pressure on the national government. Relations between the governors and the national executive have been especially important in the area of general intergovernmental studies, typified by the work of the Commission on Intergovernmental Relations and the Joint Federal-State Action Committee. In these studies, the national executive rather than Congress has taken the leadership in a co-operative exploration of federal-state problems.

4 *The Way to the White House*

Three presidents have personally addressed the Governors' Conference in regular sessions: Theodore Roosevelt in 1908, William Howard Taft in 1912, and Dwight Eisenhower in 1953 and 1957. But ordinarily presidents have not waited for an invitation from the governors. On eleven occasions the Governors' Conference has been asked by the president to a special White House meeting. While two of these meetings were mainly social, the remaining sessions were conferences about national problems.[1]

By far the most important White House meeting was the 1908 conservation conference called by Theodore Roosevelt, which has been discussed in Chapter II. After this initial encounter between the president and the governors, the White House consultations lost much of their effectiveness. When President Taft asked the governors to meet at the White House to discuss rural credits, the governors attended the conference but took no decisive action to supplement the findings of the meeting.

Woodrow Wilson, faced with postwar problems of business and labor reconstruction, assembled a different kind of conference in March, 1919. Instead of restricting his invitation to the governors, he asked a representative group of mayors to join the deliberations. The presence of

---

[1] The social functions sponsored by the presidents occurred in 1932, when Hoover held a dinner for the governors after their Richmond conference, and in 1939, when Roosevelt asked the governors to a luncheon at Hyde Park at the conclusion of their conference in Albany.

both governors and mayors severely complicated the conference. The participants were soon embroiled in severe controversies, with the result that the meeting produced no meaningful solutions to the problems set forth by President Wilson.[2]

Two White House meetings in the twenties were devoted to the issue of prohibition law enforcement. President Harding met with the governors on December 18, 1922, in an ineffectual session attended by only fourteen governors. Calvin Coolidge asked the governors to a similar prohibition meeting in 1923. Following their annual conference in West Baden, Indiana, about two-thirds of the state executives journeyed to Washington. The Coolidge conference produced an agreement on seven principles for improved law enforcement, but the generality of the agreement betrayed the deep conflict that divided the governors over the prohibition issue.

The White House consultations took on a new spirit when Franklin D. Roosevelt summoned an emergency conference of governors immediately after his inauguration in 1933. As discussed in Chapter 3, the meeting produced several resolutions supporting the Roosevelt administration and gave promise of a creative new role for the governors in national affairs. As the governors developed more of their own initiative, Roosevelt found less need to invite the governors to Washington. No more full-scale conferences occurred during the New Deal. In 1937, however, a White House luncheon for the governors was organized to discuss issues of conflicting federal-state taxation.

[2] *New York Times,* March 4, 5, 6. 1919.

3 Truman: Tension in the White House

Relations between the governors and the executive branch were none too cordial during the Truman administration. Harry Truman was the only president who did not meet with the entire Governors' Conference during his term of office. Twice he accepted invitations to address the conference, in 1945 and 1946, but on both occasions he was forced to cancel his address. Although Truman customarily sent warm messages of greeting to the governors in their annual sessions, the President's outspoken and independent conduct of national affairs left little room for consultation with the state executives.

An incident that occurred in 1947 well illustrates the stresses in Truman's relations with the governors. On January 31, 1947, readers of the *New York Times* found a front page story telling that President Truman had proposed a radical new alliance between the governors and the national executive. At the time, a soft coal strike threatened to paralyze the national economy. The *Times* reported that President Truman had polled all state governors on the course of action he should take in the strike. Moreover, said the *Times* article, the President intended to consult the governors on "any future problems of nonpartisan nature involving the convenience and necessity of the nation as a whole." The President "hopes in this way to give greater effect to the Jeffersonian concept of the Federal Union as one of delegated powers received from the sovereign States." The White House was cited as the authority for the revolutionary proposal.[3]

[3] *Ibid.*, January 31, 1947.

The governors had no time to react to the report that they were to be made partners in national policy-making, for within twenty-four hours the White House issued a denial of the *Times* story. A White House spokesman announced that if some crisis in the future "made it desirable," the President might "conceivably" seek the advice of the governors. He explained that the President had nothing to do with polling the governors on the soft coal strike. The poll had been conducted by J. A. Krug, Secretary of the Interior, with only the tacit approval of the President. The Secretary had not even shown the results of the governors' poll to the President. The poll had not sought policy advice; it had mainly asked the governors to co-operate on coal conservation measures.[4]

President Truman added to the White House announcement at his news conference on February 1. A reporter asked the President if he intended to poll governors on major policy issues in the future. The President retorted that any such story, if it came from the White House, may have come from the cooks, but not from him.[5] The remainder of President Truman's term was marked by a minimum of communication with the governors. One exception was a meeting between Truman and Democratic governors in 1950.

Eisenhower: A New Look

In contrast to his predecessor, President Eisenhower gave more attention to the governors than any president in history. But the net result of his interest was not, as

[4] *Ibid.*, February 1, 1947.
[5] *Ibid.*, February 2, 1947

some had expected at the outset of his administration, a
return of federal authority to the states. On the contrary,
federal programs continued and expanded—often with
gubernatorial support—just as they had done in the administrations of Truman and F.D.R. Yet the quality of
the relationship between the states and Washington was
greatly improved. A co-operative spirit was fostered, and
the governors were taken into the confidence of the President. The efforts of Eisenhower to encourage participation by the governors in the solution of common problems
even exceeded the initial plans of Franklin Roosevelt in
1933. The governors responded to President Eisenhower's
offers by endorsing most of the current practices of federal-
state relations.

Within months after taking office, Eisenhower asked
all governors to a high level conference at the White
House. In May, 1953, forty-four state governors and five
territorial governors gathered for a secret briefing on national and international problems by top officials of the
Eisenhower administration. Press Secretary James Hag-
erty said, "we are not inviting the Governors to come here
for just a routine briefing." [6]

It was readily apparent that the Press Secretary's description of the briefing was correct. The governors were
counseled by the Director of the Central Intelligence
Agency, the Secretary of State, the Director of the Office of
Defense Mobilization, the Director of the Civil Defense
Administration, the United Nations Representative, the
Army Chief of Staff, the Attorney General, the Secretary
of the Treasury, a Deputy Secretary of Defense, the Director of the Bureau of Budget, and several other important

[6] *Ibid.*, May 5, 1953.

officials. After two full days of briefing, the governors held
a round-table discussion with national officials on federal-
state relations. While the proceedings were kept secret, it
was apparent that the governors had never before enjoyed
such intimate acquaintance with the workings of the national executive.

The response of the governors to the briefing was en-
thusiastic. The chairman of the 1953 Governors' Conference executive committee, Allan Shivers, of Texas, reported to his colleagues that:

> The most significant progress of the past year came in the
> field of federal-state relations. The nation's Governors, in-
> dividually and collectively, were given a new high place in
> the councils of our national government. The President of
> the United States made it clear that he wanted the coopera-
> tion and assistance of the states' executives. . . . His in-
> terest and participation in the affairs of this Conference
> have done much to enhance its position and its potentiali-
> ties as a constructive force for better government.[7]

On August 4, 1953, President Eisenhower made his
first presidential address to the Governors' Conference (he
had also addressed the governors when he was Chief of
Staff). "I am here," he said, "for a very simple purpose. I
have the indestructible conviction that unless we preserve
in this country the place of the state government . . .
then we are not going to have an America as we have
known it. . . ."[8]

---

[7] *Proceedings*, 1953, p. 5.
[8] *Ibid.*, pp. 92–93. With the full support of the governors, President
Eisenhower repeated his top-level briefing session in April, 1954. Once again
the session was closed to the public. The governors were instructed on
developments in national and international policy by high administration
officials, including the Secretary of Defense; the Secretary of Health, Education, and Welfare; and the Chairman of the Council of Economic Advisers.

Briefings, expressions of good will, and sentiments about an America "as we have known it," however, were not destined to redress the balance of federal power. Eisenhower discovered this on a number of occasions when he offered the states a chance to assume greater responsibilities and was openly rebuffed.

In 1959, Eisenhower called the executive committee of the Governors' Conference to the White House to ask the states to increase their responsibility for the financing of unemployment compensation. Ordinarily, the states did handle most phases of the unemployment programs, but the recession of 1958 had drained the unemployment benefit funds of many states. The Democratic Congress had passed emergency legislation to help the distressed states and was pressing the President to agree to a continuation of the emergency program beyond its scheduled expiration date.

It was then that the President called the governors' executive committee to the White House for a special conference. While the extension bill was pending action in the Senate, the President told the governors that he favored full state responsibility in unemployment compensation. He asked the governors to seek increases in the amount and duration of state benefits, thereby avoiding, if possible, the necessity of further national action.

If the governors had accepted the President's challenge, it is possible that the action of Congress would have been stymied. But the state executives were not willing to advocate complete state autonomy in unemployment compensation. Immediately after the meeting they issued a statement supporting Eisenhower's position that the states should retain full discretion and responsibility for jobless benefits; in the same statement they said they favored "adequate Federal advances to meet emergencies where the problems of unemployment are beyond the ability of the affected state governments." [9]

Nowhere in the governors' statement did they mention the President's request that the states increase their unemployment benefit ceilings. The governors' statement was a virtual endorsement of the congressionally inspired legislation then awaiting action in the Senate. Two days after the White House conference, the Senate passed the extension bill, and the President signed the bill into law on March 31, 1959.

An even more graphic incident occurred in the summer of 1960, when Congress was debating plans for medical care of the aged. The Eisenhower administration proposed a federal grant-in-aid plan which would involve the states in the medical care program, while some legislators countered with medical care plans operated entirely by the national government and financed through the Social Security tax.

The Governors' Conference of 1960 discussed the proposals at length, and finally resolved, by a thirty to thirteen vote, to reject Eisenhower's federal-state plan in favor of the national program financed through Social Security. The Eisenhower grant-in-aid plan for medical care became law, but there were indications that it would come under heavy fire in succeeding congressional sessions. And since the governors had spoken out against the Eisenhower plan, advocates of a nationally operated program could point with telling effect to the reluctance of the states to participate.

[9] U.S., White House, *Press Release*, March 23, 1959.

Eisenhower and Intergovernmental Relations

The most memorable accomplishment in federal-state relations during the Eisenhower years was the creation of three groups: the Commission on Intergovernmental Relations, the Joint Federal-State Action Committee, and the permanent Advisory Commission on Intergovernmental Relations. President Eisenhower showed considerable interest in the aims of these groups, and his Assistant, Sherman Adams, had an influential role in their establishment before his resignation in 1958. But again, the creation of these agencies did little to change the existing balance of federal-state power.

The Commission on Intergovernmental Relations

This was the situation when Eisenhower took office in 1953: many studies had been made, mostly by private groups, state officials, or congressional committees, but practically nothing had been done to provide a systematic reassessment of federal-state relations. To correct this situation, President Eisenhower proposed the establishment of the Commission on Intergovernmental Relations in 1953. Congress promptly enacted the necessary legislation to put the commission in action.

The purpose of the commission was to study the relationship between the national government, the states, and the political subdivisions of the states "to the end that these relations may be clearly defined and the functions concerned may be allocated to their proper jurisdic-

tion." [10] The commission had no authority to follow
through on any recommendations and the life of the body
was to expire six months after the submission of its report.

The commission got off to a shaky start. Clarence E.
Manion, former Dean of the University of Notre Dame
Law School and a well-known conservative was appointed
chairman by President Eisenhower. After assuming the
chairmanship, Dean Manion continued to make heated
speeches attacking TVA and supporting the Bricker
Amendment. Some members of the commission felt that
Manion's militant dislike for the national government
prejudiced his objectivity as chairman, and they believed
his public speeches on national policies breached the pro-
prieties of his office. On February 12, 1954, Presidential
Assistant Sherman Adams, responding to complaints from
commission members and others, asked him to quit. Dean
Manion resigned on February 17, and the following day
two members of the commission resigned as a gesture of
support. Two months later, the President appointed a new
chairman, businessman Meyer Kestnbaum, whose skillful
leadership welded the group together again and contributed much to the harmonious work of the commission.

When the sixteen volumes of the commission's report
had been issued, it was clear that the group had not produced any radical proposals. The summary volume of the
report was essentially an endorsement of the status quo
in federal-state relations. While there were important suggestions about the revision of procedures in such matters
as the grant-in-aid program, the broad contours of current
practice remained unchallenged. The commission stressed
the value of state and local responsibility wherever pos-

[10] Public Law 109, Sec. 1, 67 Stat. 145 (1953).

sible, but did not suggest that the states had been over-powered by the national government, nor did it imply that the constitutional system had been perverted. The emphasis of the commission was almost entirely on federal state co-operation to smooth out rough places in existing relationships.[11]

The moderate tone of the report was sanctioned by representatives of state interests. Of the twenty-five members of the commission, seven were governors or former governors. This group was a well-organized and generally conservative bloc within the commission. Yet, while they dissented on a number of specific recommendations, all governors on the commission signed the final report.[12]

Because of the strong representation of governors on the commission, states' rights advocates could not easily criticize the report without blaming their own representatives. In an interview, one governor who had wanted an anti-national government report expressed the opinion that the commission was destined from the beginning to approve most current practices. He reasoned that a majority of the members were appointed by the President and

[11] U.S., Commission on Intergovernmental Relations, Vol. 1: *Report* (Washington: Government Printing Office, June, 1955).

[12] The members who were governors or former governors were: Alfred E Driscoll, of New Jersey, who served as vice-chairman of the commission; John S. Battle, of Virginia; Sam H. Jones, of Louisiana; Val Peterson, of Nebraska; Allan Shivers, of Texas; Dan Thornton, of Colorado; and Andrew F. Schoeppel, of Kansas. Schoeppel was serving in the Senate at the time of the commission's study.

The chairman of the commission, Meyer Kestnbaum, recognized the governors as a bloc within the commission. Addressing the Governors' Conference in 1955 just after the commission's reports had been issued, Kestnbaum observed that "although the Commission was well balanced in its representation—in that there were representatives of the Senate and the House, and local government did have a proper representation on the Commission . . . the fact is that no group was as well represented . . . as the Governors." *Proceedings*, 1955, pp. 101–102.

could not be expected to embarrass the chief executive by making harsh criticisms of the national government.

This interpretation of the commission report is subject to serious flaws. Other presidential commissions—both Hoover Commissions and the President's Committee on Administrative Management, for example—did not spare the national executive from criticism. Moreover, many of the most conservative pro-state representatives on the Commission on Intergovernmental Relations were appointed by the President. Among the fifteen presidential appointees were six of the seven governors. Some of the most outspoken pro-national members of the commission came from the Senate and House contingents, most notably Senators Hubert H. Humphrey and Wayne Morse, and Congressman John D. Dingell.

A related indication of President Eisenhower's determination to take steps to improve federal-state relations was the naming of a Deputy Assistant to the President for Intergovernmental Relations. The Deputy Assistant was responsible for liaison between the President, governors, and other officials interested in the problems of the federal system. The first person to hold the office was a former governor of Arizona, J. Howard Pyle. When Pyle resigned to accept another position, there was a reshuffling in the administrative structure. A new officer, the Deputy Assistant for Interdepartmental Affairs, acquired the duties formerly handled by Governor Pyle. The Deputy Assistant in 1960 was Robert E. Merriam.

The Joint Federal-State Action Committee

President Eisenhower's second personal address to the Governors' Conference, in 1957, was the occasion for an-

other major proposal in federal-state affairs. Moving for-
ward from the report of the Commission on Intergovernmental Relations, the President called for establishment
of a Joint Federal-State Action Committee to work out
specific plans for the reallocation of responsibilities and
taxes in the federal system. The governors promptly
adopted the suggestion.

The committee, in the President's words, would have
the following tasks:

> One—to designate functions which the states are ready
> and willing to assume and finance that are now performed
> or financed wholly or in part by the federal government;
> Two—to recommend the federal and state revenue ad-
> justments required to enable the states to assume such func-
> tions; and
> Three—to identify functions and responsibilities likely
> to require state or federal attention in the future and to
> recommend the level of state effort, or federal effort, or
> both, that will be needed to assure effective action.
> In designating the functions to be reassumed by the
> states, the committee should also specify when those func-
> tions should be assumed—the amounts by which federal
> taxes should be reduced—and increases in state revenues
> needed to support the transferred functions.[13]

Membership on the joint committee was limited to governors and members of the national executive branch.
President Eisenhower appointed a delegation of leading
national officials headed by the Secretary of the Treasury.
The Governors' Conference named as its representatives
the members of the standing committee on federal-state
relations. A governor and a national official shared the
chairmanship. No representatives of Congress or of local
government were included on the joint action committee.

[13] *Proceedings*, 1957, p. 99.

The committee began its task of sorting out national and state responsibilities with considerable caution. Avoiding the toughest problems such as employment security, public assistance, and highway construction, the committee eased into relatively less controversial matters. After making studies, the committee recommended that the national government should abandon grants in vocational education and municipal waste-treatment plant construction, giving the states full responsibility. They recommended certain revisions in the administrative relationships in urban renewal and atomic energy programs, but contemplated no change in financing. The committee also developed a more systematic plan for the administration of national disaster grants. In other policy areas such as migratory labor, flood insurance, federal lands, estate taxes, and state taxation of interstate business, the committee carried out exploratory studies.

At every turn the committee was faced with difficulties in making proposals acceptable to both state and national parties. The task of revising revenues was especially complicated. For example, to give the states revenues adequate to finance the vocational-education and waste-treatment programs (which were to be returned to the states), the committee called for a 40 per cent credit on the federal local telephone service tax to states enacting a tax equal to 40 per cent of the federal tax.[14]

The taxation proposal was seriously protested by a number of governors who foresaw imbalances arising from a blanket 40 per cent tax credit to the states. Consequently the committee reworked its proposals to allow for com-

[14] Joint Federal-State Action Committee, *Report to the President of the United States and to the Chairman of the Governors' Conference, Progress Report No. 1,* December, 1957; *Progress Report No. 2,* December, 1958.

plicated equalizing features. The revised plan provided for gradual national disengagement rather than immediate withdrawal. In almost every other policy question, the committee found it necessary to make additional studies before definite recommendations could be made.

In general, the Governors' Conference responded warily to the work of the committee. Even the first co-chairman of the committee, Governor Lane Dwinell, of New Hampshire, was unsure of the footing of the group. In 1958 he told his fellow governors:

> Nothing is easier . . . than to speculate *philosophically* on the respective roles of the various levels of government. On the other hand . . . nothing is more difficult than to attempt to spell out recommendations for the assignment or reassignment in specific areas. As is ever the case, interested groups are willing to modify or alter relationships in other fields than their own; but when it concerns a subject matter close to their own hearts, not even divine intervention is permissible without much and heavy protest.[15]

Governor Orville L. Freeman, of Minnesota, was openly critical of the joint action committee recommendations. He said:

> These recommendations have failed to generate any enthusiasm among the Governors, or, for that matter, anyone else—the White House, Congress, state legislators or public groups. In fact, the most notable aspect of the report is the heavy silence that has followed its release. The cool response is due, simply, to the fact that the recommendations are all politically and financially unrealistic. Many Governors shudder at the prospect—remote as it is—that one or more of them might in time be adopted.[16]

[15] *Proceedings,* 1958, pp. 11–12.
[16] *Ibid.,* p. 29.

Rather than repudiating the committee reports, however, the Governors' Conference supported the continuation and broadening of the group's scope. At the same time, Freeman's prophecy that few of the recommendations would be adopted was, at least during the life of the committee, quite accurate.

Although President Eisenhower incorporated several of the major proposals in his legislative recommendations, the bills made little headway in Congress. In line with one committee proposal, Congress amended the Atomic Energy Act to embody several features giving the states greater latitude in the protection of public health from radiation hazards. But this had no real relation to the structure of the federal system. On the whole, the minor modifications achieved by the joint action committee were rendered insignificant by the size of the larger issues left unsolved. To some observers, the whole affair was nothing but a ceremonial to preserve the myth that the national government could divest itself of its interest in the programs of the states.

Columnist Roscoe Drummond believed that the states had no desire to take back any functions. Surveying the work of the Joint Federal-State Action Committee, he concluded that there had been no accomplishments. "No state," he said, "has acted to take back a single function." The reasons for the failure of the states and the committee, in his view, were three: 1) the governors of the rich states were not disturbed by national encroachments; 2) other governors would like to resume certain functions but could not bring themselves to raise the taxes necessary to pay for the new functions, even if the national government abandoned the same taxes; and 3) some of the governors "would rather have the states' rights issue to talk about than to solve it." The latter governors, Drummond said, actually opposed certain services by any level of government, national or state. They veiled their opposition by claiming that the service should be performed by the states rather than the national government.[17]

The Advisory Commission on Intergovernmental Relations

In the long run, the most important development in federal-state relations during the Eisenhower administration may prove to be the creation, in 1959, of a permanent Advisory Commission on Intergovernmental Relations. The establishment of the commission was supported by the Governors' Conference and other groups of state and local officials.[18]

The new advisory commission embodied many of the functions recommended by study groups in the past. As a

---

[17] *New York Herald Tribune,* August 5, 1959.

[18] The groundwork for the advisory commission was laid in the House Intergovernmental Relations Subcommittee of the Committee on Government Operations. For four years, the House subcommittee conducted special studies and held national and regional hearings on federal-state-local relations.

The subcommittee, called the Fountain committee after its chairman, Cong. L. H. Fountain, of North Carolina, issued a series of preliminary documents. The most important were U.S., Congress, House, Committee on Government Operations, *Federal-State-Local Relations, Federal Grants-In-Aid, Thirtieth Report,* 85 Cong., 2 sess., House Report No. 2533; and *Establishing an Advisory Commission on Intergovernmental Relations,* 86 Cong., 1 sess., House Report No. 742.

See also U.S., Congress, House, Intergovernmental Relations Subcommittee and Senate, Committee on Government Operations, *To Establish an Advisory Commission on Intergovernmental Relations, Joint Hearings, H.R. 6904, H.R. 6905, and S. 2026,* 86 Cong., 1 sess., June 16–22, 1959. In these hearings, two governors testified in support of the legislation (the three bills were identical), and eighteen other governors filed letters generally endorsing the creation of an advisory commission.

permanent, statutory body, the commission was charged
with responsibility to:

(1) bring together representatives of the Federal, State
and local governments for the consideration of common
problems;

(2) provide a forum for discussing the administration
and coordination of Federal grant and other programs requiring intergovernmental cooperation;

(3) give critical attention to the conditions and controls
involved in the administration of Federal grant programs;

(4) make available technical assistance to the executive
and legislative branches of the Federal Government in the
review of proposed legislation to determine its overall effect
on the Federal system;

(5) encourage discussion and study at an early stage of
emerging public problems that are likely to require intergovernmental cooperation;

(6) recommend, within the framework of the Constitution, the most desirable allocation of governmental functions, responsibilities, and revenues among the several
levels of government; and

(7) recommend methods of coordinating and simplify-
ing tax laws and administrative practices to achieve a more
orderly and less competitive fiscal relationship between the
levels of government and to reduce the burden of com-
pliance for taxpayers.[19]

Membership on the advisory commission differs mark-
edly from the Joint Federal-State Action Committee. The
members of the advisory commission are drawn from
private life, the House and Senate, the executive branch,
governors, state legislators, mayors, and county officials.

[19] Public Law 86–380, Sec. 2, 73 Stat. 703 (1959). After the enactment of this
legislation, the old Joint Federal-State Action Committee, which had no
statutory basis, voted to discontinue operation and turn all records over to
the new commission.

The cosmopolitan membership of the commission potentially changed the power of the governors in the conduct of intergovernmental negotiations. Their representation on the advisory commission is smaller than it was on either the Kestnbaum commission or the joint action committee. Only four governors are members of the twenty-six member commission. They are appointed by the president from a panel of eight or more governors submitted by the Governors' Conference. Four mayors and three county officials counterbalance the presence of governors and state legislators.

One former governor expressed the fear in an interview that the composition of the new commission was an attempt to "outflank the governors" with local government officials and state legislators. More time will have to elapse before an evaluation of the commission's bias can be made. Supporters of state interests took solace, however, from the fact that the first chairman of the Advisory Commission was Frank Bane, former director of the Council of State Governments and Secretary-Treasurer of the Governors' Conference, a man well versed in the problems of state government.

Aside from the direct communication between the governors and the presidents, there has been a steady interchange between governors and subordinate officials in the national executive branch. Spaced fairly evenly through the history of the Governors' Conference, forty high-ranking officials in the executive branch had addressed the conference. One Vice-President, Richard Nixon, appeared before the governors in 1956. Cabinet members to appear have included the Secretaries of State, War, Navy, Treasury, Agriculture, Defense, and Health,

Education, and Welfare. Lesser officials—budget directors, national guard officials, and welfare administrators, for example—have spoken at governors' sessions. In addition, an undetermined number of national executive officials have attended the conference as guests without responsibilities on the formal program.

In the first twenty years of the conference, national executive officials usually spoke to the governors in innocuous platitudes. Since the New Deal, national officials have usually been serious, specific, and candid in their speeches before the governors. Often a speech would be a defense of a controversial administration policy or an explanation of a new federal-state program. On several occasions the governors relentlessly pressed the speakers for answers to states' complaints. In some cases the governors achieved results with their questions: national officials would promise to investigate bothersome national policies or to seek some change.

Governors' Conference committees have met frequently in Washington with representatives of the executive branch to work out detailed policies in federal-state relations. Special delegations of governors have met with Defense Department officials concerning national guard policy, with civil defense officials, and with many other groups of national administrators.

6

The International
Dimension

A FEW decades ago it would have seemed incongruous
—if not wholly inappropriate—for state governors
to be concerned officially with foreign affairs. Yet in recent
years delegations of governors have conferred with heads
of foreign states in Buenos Aires, Rio, and the Kremlin,
while a steady flow of foreign policy resolutions has issued
from the annual Governors' Conferences. While these
actions have had only a minor influence in the international scheme of things, they notably alter the traditional
role of the state executives.

In a sense, the addition of this international aspect to
the daily concern of governors is merely a reflection of the
growing interdependency of all nations on a complex
planet. What happens in Leopoldville or Havana may ultimately affect the states as much as what happens in Sacra-
mento or Hartford, and modern governors who ignore international developments do so at their own peril. But in
a more particular sense, the governors have discovered that
American foreign policies tangibly affect internal state
affairs. The economy of a state may be bolstered or hin-
dered by federal immigration policies, tariffs, and export

licensing restrictions. The financial burden of national defense and foreign aid has placed a direct strain on the ability of states to find sources of revenue for their own programs. Governors have felt the pinch of international necessity and they have stepped up their interest in foreign affairs.

As careful students of the federal Constitution, state governors have not questioned the right of the national government to control foreign policy. But they have devised informal means to express their opinions, to exert their influence, and to inform themselves about conditions in the world arena.

The End of Isolationism

The governors avoided discussion of foreign affairs until the rude facts of international conflict forced their way into the deliberations of the Governors' Conference with the outbreak of World War II in Europe. For a brief time, some governors held to the position that the United States should stay out of European and Asian affairs. Governor Lloyd C. Stark, of Missouri, chairman of the executive committee in 1940, indicated in an opening statement to the 1940 conference that governors should mold public opinion against any direct involvement in foreign conflict. He nevertheless advocated a militant program of national defense and admitted that international events had subordinated many of the domestic problems of the governors. His statement against foreign involvement was one of the last of its kind in conference sessions.[1]

[1] *Proceedings*, 1940, pp. 3–6. In postwar years, Governor J. Bracken Lee, of Utah, was the most outspoken isolationist in the conference. His views received courteous but perfunctory attention from his colleagues.

By 1941 the international situation had grown worse. The governors were preoccupied with problems of national defense and foreign policy and showed little disposition to avoid international involvement. Five months before the Japanese attack on Pearl Harbor, Governor Charles A. Sprague, of Oregon, spoke to the 1941 conference on the necessity of American participation in Asiatic affairs. Secretary of the Navy Frank Knox proposed to the governors that the United States Navy should be used to clear the Atlantic shipping lanes of German submarines, while Malcolm MacDonald, High Commissioner in Canada for the United Kingdom, analyzed the position of Great Britain at that crucial juncture in the European war. A year later, when the United States was at war, the governors heard addresses from the British Ambassador, the Viscount Halifax; the Chinese Ambassador, Dr. Hu Shih; and the Netherlands Ambassador, Dr. Alexander Loudon.

The governors' first formal sortie into foreign affairs came in 1943, when the governors were addressed by Joseph E. Davies, former American Ambassador to Russia, on the efforts of the Soviet Union in the war. His account of the heroism of the Soviet people was coupled with a plea for renewed friendship with the Soviet nation at the close of the war. Of the governors, whom he called "lovers of peace and great Americans," Davies asked co-operation in creating a public opinion which would bolster the confidence of the allied nations. "Russia, Britain, China, or any other of the United Nations," he said, "should not be alienated by intolerance or little criticisms of one against the other." [2]

[2] *Ibid.*, 1943, p. 77.

Heeding the Ambassador's plea, Governor Raymond E. Baldwin, of Connecticut, a Republican, introduced a resolution which praised the bravery of the Russians in their resistance to German invasion and extended "warm greetings," "keen admiration," and "heartiest congratulations" to the Russian people. The conference adopted the resolution with unanimous approval.[3] The governors' statement carefully avoided an endorsement of the Soviet system and did not call for any specific action by the national government. The resolution primarily sought to create an atmosphere of support for the people of the Soviet Union in their fight against Hitler.

In the light of postwar enmity between Russia and the United States, many governors might have wished later that they had chosen a different topic for their first venture into foreign policy. No protests were lodged against the governors' action, however, and the precedent of foreign policy resolutions was established. Most important, the statement addressed to the Soviet Union indicated a new temper among the chief executives and a willingness to go beyond the boundaries of domestic policy.

The new outlook of the governors was confirmed when the governors assembled in July, 1945. By then, the Germans were defeated and Japanese defenses were crumbling. The San Francisco conference had completed its work on a charter for the United Nations. Fresh from that conference was Commander Harold Stassen, former Governor of Minnesota, former chairman of the Conference executive committee, and a member of the American delegation to San Francisco. He was asked to report to the governors on the work of the United Nations Charter conference.

[3] *Ibid.,* p. 146

Stassen was convinced that isolationism was an impossible course for the United States to follow in the postwar era. International relations had been changed irrevocably, and only the active participation of the United States in world affairs could assure world peace. In Stassen's view, the change in international relations was laden with implications for the state chief executives. He insisted that henceforth the governors would have to give increased time to the analysis of world problems and would have to become spokesmen on international problems to the people of the states. The breakdown of isolationism meant that the foreign policy of the United States could no longer be the exclusive product of the State Department, the President, and the Senate. Rather, postwar foreign policy, in his view, would have to be made collectively, through the processes of public opinion. Stassen therefore urged the chief executives "to exercise to an increasing degree in your state a positive leadership in the world policy of this country." [4]

Above all, Stassen believed that prompt Senate ratification of the United Nations charter was a critical necessity. Without debate, and with unanimous support, the governors accepted Stassen's challenge by resolving to favor the entry of the United States into the United Nations Organization. "We endorse the United Nations Charter, as drafted," said the governors, "and urge its prompt approval by the United States Senate so that the United States can lead the way in this greatest of man's efforts." [5]

---

[4] *Ibid.*, 1945, pp. 90–91.

[5] *Ibid.*, p. 223. During the 1945 meeting, thirty-seven of the governors acted outside the official bounds of the Governors' Conference to petition President Truman to take up the question of Palestine at his Potsdam conference with Stalin and Churchill. Stressing that their petition was a personal undertaking rather than an official action of the conference, the governors said: "We believe that the time has come when concrete measures must be taken

The efforts of the governors were only a small part of the
nationwide movement to win public support for the
United Nations. The willingness of the governors to speak
out on international affairs was symptomatic of the rejection of isolationism by the American people.

Bipartisan foreign policy received a boost from the governors during the years of the controversial Eightieth Congress. While Democratic and Republican internationalists
in Congress were fighting to prevent serious schisms in the
united front of American foreign policy, the Governors'
Conference of 1947 asserted its conviction "that the foreign policy of this country transcends in importance all
partisan, personal, or political considerations and should
be at all times an American foreign policy. . . ." [6] The
governors avoided a more specific endorsement of administration policy. The *New York Times* reported that the
bipartisanship resolution was approved only after the re-
moval of phraseology that could imply conference endorsement of the Truman Doctrine and the Marshall
Plan.[7]

When the governors assembled at Colorado Springs in
1949, the reluctance to endorse specific programs had van-
ished. In a three-point resolution, the forty-first annual
meeting advocated 1) continued support of the United Nations as essential to peaceful settlement of international

to open the doors of Palestine to Jewish mass immigration and coloniza-
tion. . . ." Leaders in the petition were Governor Thomas E. Dewey, of
New York; Raymond E. Baldwin, of Connecticut; Herbert B. Maw, of Utah;
Maurice J. Tobin, of Massachusetts; and J. Howard McGrath, of Rhode
Island; a bipartisan group of two Republicans and three Democrats. Gov-
ernors from all parts of the nation supported the petition. *New York Times,*
July 5, 1945.

[6] *Proceedings,* 1947, p. 278.
[7] *New York Times,* July 17, 1947.

disputes; 2) continuation and adequate financing of the Marshall Plan, which they deemed of great importance to the political and economic life of Europe and the "continuance of free institutions in that frontier of democracy"; and 3) prompt Senate approval of the North Atlantic Pact, which had been agreed to in Washington only two months before the 1949 Governors' Conference. The governors also called upon the Senate to take all necessary action to give the North Atlantic Pact full force and effect.[8]

Whatever foothold isolationism may have had in the Governors' Conference was removed by the governors' decisive assertion of internationalist convictions. The United Nations, the Marshall Plan, and the North Atlantic Pact were the cornerstones of what has been called the revolution in American foreign policy. The Governors' Conference gave unanimous approval to all three undertakings.

The Assessment of World Problems

The new interest of state governors in foreign affairs was nurtured by exposure to the opinions of experts in international politics. In the postwar years it became a regular order of business to have highly placed foreign policy and military officials appear before the Governors' Conference. Often the discussions were off the record. At other times the speeches were public and, consequently, more gentle in tone than some of the private addresses.

Five times between 1943 and 1951, General George C. Marshall joined the governors in their annual meetings to brief them on world affairs. In the first three meetings he

[8] *Proceedings*, 1949, p. 184.

was present as Chief of Staff of the U.S. Army; in 1947 he came to the governors as Secretary of State under President Truman. In 1951 he was present as an elder statesman in international affairs.

On two occasions—in 1944 and 1945—Chief of Naval Operations Ernest J. King accompanied General Marshall in the governors' off-the-record briefing session. In 1946, General of the Army Dwight Eisenhower, then Chief of Staff, and Fleet Admiral Chester Nimitz, then Chief of Naval Operations, gave off-the-record information to the governors.

Foreign policy discussions were frequent in the postwar decade. Edward R. Murrow and Dorothy Thompson discussed prevailing international conditions at the governors' meeting in 1948. General Walter Bedell Smith, former Ambassador to Russia, addressed the governors about Soviet-American relations in 1949. Paul G. Hoffman, head of the Economic Cooperation Administration, appeared before the conference in 1950 to explain the progress of the Marshall Plan.

President Truman recognized the governors' interest in foreign policy in his message to them in 1950. "I am pleased to note," he said, "that several sessions on your . . . program are devoted to foreign affairs and the work of the Economic Cooperation Administration. This is an encouraging development. In order to preserve world peace, there must be an informed opinion on the great issues of our foreign policy." [9] He refuted the idea that foreign policy was made entirely in Washington and welcomed the participation of governors in the quest for

[9] *Proceedings*, 1950, p. 9.

world peace. In view of Truman's previous disdain for the opinions of governors, mentioned in Chapter 5, the state executives may have sensed a note of irony in the message of the President.

President Truman's chief representative at the 1950 conference was Secretary of State Dean Acheson. He appeared before the governors during a period of intense public criticism of the State Department. Republicans in Washington were clamoring for the resignation of the Secretary, and their demands were supported by no small number of Democrats. The public press was filled with controversy over the Voice of America program, communists in the State Department, employment of aliens in American embassies, and competition between domestic industry and imported commodities. Because of these issues, the governors were particularly anxious to question Acheson.

For the first time, the governors arranged a round-table discussion on foreign affairs, with Acheson as the principal speaker and target of questions. After a general comment on the state of the world, the Secretary opened the meeting to questions from the floor. A volley of interrogations from the governors covered practically every phase of controversy over American foreign policy.

The governors demonstrated by their questions that they were well informed about foreign affairs. Despite the fact that many of the questions were designed to put the Secretary in the worst possible light, Acheson held his ground before the governors and answered questions with agility. It was later revealed that the Secretary had been prepared for some of the rougher quizzing in a pre-dawn session with the 1950 executive committee chairman, William Preston Lane, Jr., of Maryland.[10]

After Acheson's turbulent round-table session, foreign policy discussions assumed a calmer air but still occupied a position of importance on conference agenda. John Foster Dulles (then ambassador) in 1951 addressed the governors on the negotiation of the Japanese Peace Treaty. Sir Roger Makins, the British Ambassador, spoke to the governors in 1955. An important briefing session on the status of the North Atlantic Treaty Organization was provided in 1956 by General Alfred M. Gruenther, then Supreme Allied Commander in Europe. International problems were again a principal theme in 1958, when United Nations Secretary-General Dag Hammarskjold assessed the ability of the United Nations to establish peace in the midst of international conflict.

Mature Internationalism

With the selection of Governor LeRoy Collins, of Florida, as chairman of the conference executive committee in 1958, the Governors' Conference entered a new phase of activity in international relations. Governor Collins was determined from the outset of his administration as chairman that the conference should pursue a vigorous course of action on several fronts.

In an article written for International News Service, Collins charted a new path for the state governors. He observed that the association of governors had grown year by year until it had attained a stature "as a major instrument of governmental influence." He proposed essentially a

[10] Interview with Governor William Preston Lane, Jr., November 19, 1959.

four point program; first, the governors would work for a realignment of federal-state responsibilities; second, the governors would explore their own states to determine which services the states needed to undertake in a changing world; third, the executive committee would undertake a more active role in the interim between meetings; and fourth, he said, "I think it is likely that the governors conference will concern itself more with our nation's foreign policy."

The reason for an increase of gubernatorial interest in foreign affairs, Governor Collins explained, was that defense expenditure, the largest single item in the federal budget, was related directly to the conduct of the cold war. While he had no doubt that the conduct of foreign policy remained solely in the hands of the federal government, he believed that such policy had an immediate bearing on the ability of the states to serve their own people. "Because of this," he said,

> I hope we will be able to contribute in some way toward the relaxation of international tensions and the development of the kind of American foreign policy which not only will allow this country—through all levels of its government—to serve more fully the American people, but which will also enable Americans to live in peace and good will with their fellow men.[11]

Events quickly revealed the new determination of the governors to take part in international politics, for the conference launched a series of newsworthy innovations in foreign affairs. A major development was a study trip to the Soviet Union by nine governors representing the executive committee of the Governors' Conference. Its pur-

[11] *Tampa Morning Tribune,* May 23, 1958.

pose was to study state and local institutions in the Soviet Union, with a possible view to establishing a "systematic research relationship" between the Soviet republics and the Council of State Governments. The trip was further designed to generate interest in state and local levels of foreign governments among the general public, and eventually to afford Soviet officials an opportunity to study state and local government in the United States.[12]

When news of the trip was published there were varied public reactions. One group, the Committee for the Preservation of the Constitution, circulated a petition to be sent to Senator James Eastland, Chairman of the Senate Judiciary Committee. The resolution contended that the nine governors, by proposing to study Soviet government, had "openly admitted their lack of . . . faith in our constitutional government, by seeking instruction in an un-American dictatorship." The petition urged the Judiciary Committee to prevent such an invasion of foreign ideas by giving the governors one-way transportation to Russia and permanently canceling their passports so that they could not re-enter the United States.[13]

The ten-thousand-mile trip took place in the summer of 1959 amid wide press and radio coverage. In the course of their travels through the Soviet Union, the governors

[12] The trip was proposed by the Institute of International Education and financed by the Rockefeller Brothers Fund and the Alfred P. Sloan Foundation. A budget of $32,280 was requested for the trip of nine governors and seven other persons.

After substitutions to fill the places of executive committee members who were unable to attend, the entourage consisted of Democrats LeRoy Collins, of Florida; Robert B. Meyner, of New Jersey; Stephen L. R. McNichols, of Colorado; and Luther H. Hodges of North Carolina; and Republicans George D. Clyde, of Utah; Cecil H. Underwood, of West Virginia; William G. Stratton, of Illinois; John E. Davis, of North Dakota; Robert E. Smylie, of Idaho; and assistants, consultants, and representatives of educational groups.

[13] Undated petition, filed at office of the Council of State Governments.

held a three-and-a-half-hour conference with Soviet Premier Nikita Khrushchev and a conference with Soviet Deputy Premier Anastas Mikoyan. But the governors were primarily concerned with the operation of Soviet government at the level of the republics. In all, the governors visited five Soviet republics and conferred with hundreds of Soviet officials.

The fruits of the trip were summarized in nine separate reports to the Governors' Conference in August, 1959. The reports were studious in tone, covering a variety of subjects such as the communist party, agriculture, the habits and culture of the Russian people, and the operation of Soviet government. In a general statement regarding the tour, the nine governors agreed on several major points, including the impression that the Soviet Union had made "substantial progress" in the development of the country. They felt that there was no indication that the Soviet people entertained any desire to abandon their system of government. They concluded that means for increased international understanding, improved friendship, and factual exchange of information between the United States and the Soviet Union were needed.

International political developments hovered in the background of the governors' tour. The summer of 1959 was the time of President Eisenhower's momentous decision to invite Premier Nikita Khrushchev to visit the United States. Upon their return, the nine governors visited the White House to report to the President and to urge him to go to the Soviet Union and to invite Soviet Premier Khrushchev to the United States.

As it happened, Vice-President Nixon was also conducting a tour of the Soviet Union when the governors made

their report to the President. In a radio-television broad-
cast in Moscow on August 1, the Vice-President asserted
that further exchange visits between the two nations would
be desirable, but did not specify that Khrushchev should
come to the United States. In a final news conference in
Moscow on August 2, the Vice-President said that he believed the Soviet Premier should "at some time visit the
United States." [14]

Three days after the governors had visited the White
House, and while Vice-President Nixon was in Poland on
his way home to the United States, President Eisenhower
held an unexpected news conference and announced that
the Soviet Premier would visit the United States. The
news was released while the Governors' Conference was in
session at San Juan, Puerto Rico, and the governors reacted to the President's announcement in a variety of ways.
Governor Ernest F. Hollings, of South Carolina, wanted
the governors to disclaim any credit for bringing the Soviet Premier to American shores. "I hope the President's
action was not based on the Governors' recommendation,"
he said. "I don't believe the Governors should start for-
mulating foreign policy." [15]

Governor Nelson Rockefeller, of New York, however,
gave major credit to the governors for the move. "It is a
great tribute to the Governors' Conference and their concern over international affairs," he said, "that their recommendation to the President has been approved. It shows
the expanding influence of the role that the Governors
are playing." [16]

[14] *New York Times,* August 2, 3, 1959.
[15] *Ibid.,* August 4, 1959.
[16] Observers did not fail to note the political significance of Governor
Rockefeller's outspoken praise for the governors. Rockefeller, then the major

While the governors debated over the extent of their influence in the President's decision, it appeared that the estimation of *Baltimore Sun* correspondent Gerald Griffin most accurately described the actual role of the governors. "To a considerable extent," he reported, ". . . the governors had helped to create a favorable atmosphere for the proposed exchange of visits between President Eisenhower and Khrushchev." [17] For it is highly unlikely that the decision to invite Khrushchev was made on the spur of the moment, and preliminary negotiations presumably were in progress for some time before the governors had visited the White House. But the governors' public support of the visit gave the President a good opportunity to make public the historic decision.

Several months later, the Governors' Conference was host to a number of their counterparts from the Soviet republics. The Russian officials toured the United States in the face of several heated anti-communist demonstrations. But this exchange of visits was the last significant exchange that took place during the Eisenhower Administration, for Soviet-American relations worsened after the American U-2 spy plane was shot down in Russia and the proposed visit of President Eisenhower was canceled.

A year after the governors had invaded the Soviet Union they turned their attention to matters south of the border.

---

unannounced contender against Vice-President Nixon for the Republican presidential nomination in 1960, made no mention of any influence that Nixon might have had in the decision. Don Erwin of the *New York Herald Tribune* reported that "Mr. Rockefeller's failure to mention the Vice-President may have been accidental. Or, from word that is circulating from the Rockefeller camp to the many other Governors who are closely attentive to the only serious Republican Presidential prospect in their midst, it was no accident." *New York Herald Tribune*, August 4, 1959.

[17] *Baltimore Sun*, August 4, 1959.

Urged on by governors who were particularly concerned about problems in Latin America—most notably Nelson Rockefeller, of New York—the Governors' Conference conducted a two-week trip of Argentina and Brazil after the elections of November, 1960. Twenty-eight governors made the trip, accompanied by the usual contingent of newsmen and staff assistants. They flew, rode, and walked into all corners of the two Latin American nations. They submitted to the customary niceties of formal receptions and dinners with ranking government officials, but many of the governors escaped from the confines of guided tours whenever possible to talk to Latin Americans in all walks of life.

The governors wanted, and got, a good glimpse of the revolutionary movements in the southern hemisphere. Pro-Castro students demonstrated against North American imperialism as the governors filed out of their hotels. Government leaders cast aside pleasantries to explain the urgent crises of the burgeoning Latin nations. The governors saw poverty, but they also saw the awesome potential of Brazil and Argentina. When they returned home, they made clear their determination to press the national government for prompt and effective action in South America. The state executives also regarded the trip as an important display of national unity on the heels of a bitter presidential election. Republican Governor Harold Handley, of Indiana, summed up the feelings of many governors when he said that the trip "has proven to Latin America that our country comes first and political parties second. This display of unity . . . will certainly have an impact on the thinking of our friends in the southern half of the hemisphere." [18]

[18] *Denver Post,* November 29, 1960.

Everywhere the governors turned, it seemed, they added an international flavor to their work. Their 1959 conference was held for the first time outside the continental limits of the United States, in the Commonwealth of Puerto Rico. In that Caribbean setting, the governors grappled seriously with the problems of Latin America. A year later the governors shifted the scene to Glacier Park, Montana, near the Canadian border, where they discussed Canadian-American relations with John G. Diefenbaker, Prime Minister of Canada. As Governor Collins remarked, the international break-through by the governors indicated "a new direction and a new dimension for the Governors' Conference." "More and more attention," he observed, "is being focused on the Governors' Conference—as a Conference, rather than as a collection of individual Governors. It is becoming increasingly a force, in its own right, on the national governmental scene." [19]

In the entire history of the Governors' Conference prior to World War II, the governors had never been involved in international affairs. In the First World War, the governors had discussed international military developments primarily in terms of domestic requirements of production. After 1943, the conference moved gradually into foreign affairs until it reached a state of full-blown involvement with the trips to the Soviet Union and Latin America.

Aside from a brief flourish of isolationism before Pearl Harbor, the governors' actions in foreign policy have had one outstanding characteristic: the Governors' Conference has supported increased American involvement in international affairs. While some governors have believed that withdrawal from foreign entanglements would re-

[19] *State Government*, Vol. XXXII (Autumn, 1959), pp 220–21.

move many threats to the financial and legal standing of the states, they have not attempted to keep the national government out of international politics. Even when far-reaching commitment was required—as in the case of the North Atlantic Treaty Organization, the Marshall Plan, and the United Nations—the Governors' Conference has favored participation.

The concrete influence of the governors on foreign policy has been decidedly modest. Their activities have been confined mainly to the realm of resolutions, speeches, and good-will tours. In contrast to their aggressive participation in domestic national policies, their involvement in international affairs is distinctly subordinate. And the governors have kept out of policy disputes or concerted drives to cut foreign aid that it would have seemed logical for them to enter: the Governors' Conference had no discussions and passed no resolutions on the controversial Bricker Amendment which was proposed to limit the treaty-making power of the national government. But it is significant that the governors have been willing to break out of the confines of their traditional role to take a part—however minor—in the shaping of international affairs.

7

The Partisans

"ONE MIGHT as well expect a gathering of Junior Leaguers to pass up talk of romance," noted one observer of the Governors' Conference, "as to expect forty-eight robust Governors to get together and shy away from politics." [1] Indeed, the governors are old and seasoned hands in the control of national party politics, and a goodly share of their time is devoted to running the Republican and Democratic parties. Ever since the Civil War, governors have been eminent contenders for the presidency and have customarily been chief wire-pullers in the national conventions.

The position of governors as national party leaders and presidential contenders has been challenged seriously in recent presidential elections. To assess the magnitude of this challenge, this chapter scrutinizes the partisan activity of the governors at their annual conferences, while the next chapter ventures on to a broader plane, examining the problems of the governors in competition with senators and other national figures in the presidential sweepstakes.

[1] Edward T. Folliard, in *State Government*, Vol. XXXI (Summer, 1958), p. 175.

Governors as Presidential Candidates

For many decades, history has been kind to the state executives. As the governorship matured into a significant position, the governors attracted more and more attention as potential candidates for the presidency. In the early years of the republic many presidents served as governors at some time during their careers but did not come to the White House directly from the governorship. Monroe, Van Buren, Tyler, Polk, and Johnson were once state governors. Jefferson was a revolutionary war governor of Virginia, Jackson had been territorial governor of Florida, and William Henry Harrison was territorial governor of Indiana.

The nomination of Horatio Seymour by the Democrats in 1868, however, marked the first time that an incumbent governor was selected by a party convention. The fact that Seymour had been an outstanding governor of New York was a primary factor in choosing him to oppose Grant. In 1876, the rise of governors as presidential candidates was evident when both major parties nominated sitting governors, Tilden of New York and Hayes of Ohio.

From 1876 onward, the state chief executives held a secure and pre-eminent place in national politics. Cleveland's record as governor of New York had much to do with putting him in the White House. McKinley drew national attention while he occupied the governor's chair in Ohio. Theodore Roosevelt was swept into the vice-presidency from the governorship of New York, ultimately to become president.

After the Governors' Conference was established in

1908, state governors continued to dominate party presidential nominations. As indicated in Figure 2, four out of ten Republicans and five out of nine Democrats who have since been nominated for president were governors. In the Republican party, the presidential standard was carried by Governors Hughes, Coolidge, Landon, and Dewey, while the Democrats turned to Wilson, Cox, Smith, Roosevelt, and Stevenson. Of the governors, only Hughes and Coolidge were not in office at the time of their nomination. Hughes was on the Supreme Court when he was chosen. Coolidge received the vice-presidential nomination when he was governor in 1920 and moved into the presidency after the death of Harding.

The vice-presidency garnered its own share of governors as candidates. Republicans Coolidge, Bricker, and Warren, and Democrats Marshall, Charles W. Bryan and Robinson claimed experience as governors as part of their qualification for the nomination. With the exception of Joseph T. Robinson, who served briefly as governor of Arkansas before going on to a distinguished career in the United States Senate, the governors who became vice-presidential candidates after 1908 were in office at the time of their first nomination.

Third parties placed particular reliance on governors as nominees. The Progressives chose Theodore Roosevelt and Hiram Johnson in 1912. The 1924 Progressive presidential candidate was Robert M. LaFollette, who had been governor of Wisconsin at the turn of the century. The Dixiecrats entered two governors against the regular Democrats in 1948: Governor J. Strom Thurmond of South Carolina as presidential nominee, and Governor Fielding Wright of Mississippi for vice-president.

PRESIDENTIAL AND VICE-PRESIDENTIAL NOMINEES, 1908–1960

(STATE GOVERNORS IN CAPITAL LETTERS; ASTERISK DENOTES WINNER)

REPUBLICAN	DEMOCRAT
1908 William H. Taft *	William J. Bryan
James S. Sherman	John W. Kern
1912 William H. Taft	WOODROW WILSON *
James S. Sherman	THOMAS R. MARSHALL
1916 CHARLES EVANS HUGHES	WOODROW WILSON *
Charles W. Fairbanks	THOMAS R. MARSHALL
1920 Warren G. Harding *	JAMES M. COX
CALVIN COOLIDGE	Franklin D. Roosevelt
1924 CALVIN COOLIDGE *	John W. Davis
Charles G. Dawes	CHARLES W. BRYAN
1928 Herbert Hoover *	ALFRED E. SMITH
Charles Curtis	JOSEPH T. ROBINSON
1932 Herbert Hoover	FRANKLIN D. ROOSEVELT *
Charles Curtis	John N. Garner
1936 ALFRED M. LANDON	FRANKLIN D. ROOSEVELT *
Frank Knox	John N. Garner
1940 Wendell L. Willkie	FRANKLIN D. ROOSEVELT *
Charles L. McNary	Henry A. Wallace
1944 THOMAS E. DEWEY	FRANKLIN D. ROOSEVELT *
JOHN W. BRICKER	Harry S. Truman
1948 THOMAS E. DEWEY	Harry S. Truman *
EARL WARREN	Alben W. Barkley
1952 Dwight D. Eisenhower *	ADLAI E. STEVENSON
Richard M. Nixon	John J. Sparkman
1956 Dwight D. Eisenhower *	ADLAI E. STEVENSON
Richard M. Nixon	Estes Kefauver
1960 Richard M. Nixon	John F. Kennedy *
Henry Cabot Lodge	Lyndon B. Johnson

MAJOR THIRD PARTY CANDIDATES

1912 THEODORE ROOSEVELT (Progressive)
HIRAM JOHNSON
1924 ROBERT M. LAFOLLETTE (Progressive)
Burton Wheeler
1948 J. STROM THURMOND (Dixiecrat)
FIELDING WRIGHT

Figure 2

Conference Politics

The governors were established in national party politics long before Theodore Roosevelt thought of calling a Governors' Conference, but the existence of the conference gave the governors an added opportunity to promote their national aspirations. Most governors are leaders of their state parties and are influential in casting a state's delegation votes at the national conventions. A presidentially-minded governor finds, in a single meeting, most of the political leaders who could give him the nomination. Thus the conferences are perennially the scene of intensive backstage political maneuvering, cajoling, and pledging.

For the governor who wants to be president, the conference has also been a convenient and effective podium for national publicity. Over one hundred professional correspondents customarily attend the meeting, representing most leading newspapers, news services, radio-television networks, and such magazines as *Time, Life, Newsweek,* and *Saturday Evening Post*. Except for national conventions, few public gatherings draw such widespread press attendance, and on practically no other occasion can the governors bask in such extensive national publicity.

The press has long been aware of the significance of the conference for political news. "Governors are usually the controlling powers in Presidential nominating conventions," noted the *New York Times* in 1956. "Therefore the best political weather station in a Presidential year is the annual Governors' Conference, which comes before the conventions."[2] To a tongue-in-cheek British

[2] *New York Times,* July 1, 1956.

correspondent, the partisan side of the conference was all that really mattered.

> There has recently been concluded in the United States an annual ritual which gathers the Governors of most of the forty-eight states in one place to talk politics. These Governors, it should be noted, represent both the Republican and Democratic parties and it is mainly because, politically, they dominate their states that their assembly has importance. . . .

> While the Governors ostensibly discuss matters which are of interest to them as state executives, the real reason for their gathering is to make them accessible as a group to political reporters. They do everything they can to interest and attract journalists and, long after interstate resolutions on highways, hospitals, and what not are forgotten, the sum of their political judgments is being weighed against the current party scene.[3]

Members of the working press have had a tendency to overplay the partisan aspects of conference activity, overshadowing the less exciting developments in policy formation. In a tense presidential countdown, reporters may seize on the chance comments of a governor as he passes through a hotel lobby and blow it up into a major political story. To give the conference political reportage a semblance of order, many governors have resorted to formal press conferences during the meetings.

This is not to say that presidential aspirants publicly trumpet their availability at the conferences. Each governor uses different techniques, but in general the maneuvers are subtly calculated to bring a governor's qualifications into national focus. A review of the activities of

---

[3] "Political Rites," *Economist*, August 27, 1955, pp. 695–96.

several outstanding governors will illustrate the presidential strategy employed at the conference.

C The Rise of Roosevelt

One of the greatest political wizards of the Governors' Conference was Franklin D. Roosevelt. For four years prior to his presidential nomination in 1932, Roosevelt enhanced his national reputation at the annual meetings. The natural advantages were in his favor from the beginning. As a governor representing the party out of power, he was in a position to criticize the Hoover administration. He was governor of the state with the largest electoral vote in the nation. And he spoke with a charm and enthusiasm that attracted attention during the critical years of the depression.

Each year during his term as governor, Roosevelt managed to appear as a principal speaker at the annual conference. And each year the reporters present would headline his comments. By 1930 it was becoming more apparent that Roosevelt was a strong but unannounced possibility for the Democratic nomination. When the governors assembled in Salt Lake City, the Republican mayor, in welcoming the state executives, made a not-too-subtle reference to Roosevelt's presidential prospects. The governors broke into resounding applause, while Roosevelt sat there silently. Later, in an aside, a reporter heard F.D.R. remark, "I felt like crawling under my desk."

Roosevelt may have blushed appropriately, but he was undeterred in making an important play for national attention during the 1930 meeting. As a main speaker, he

moved aggressively into the controversial topic of unemployment and old age insurance. The *New York Times*
reported that the speech was a "sensation," and said that
Roosevelt "received more than casual mention as a Presidential possibility and was made the object of a demon-
stration of greater warmth and volume than any of the
others at the opening session." [4]

Behind the scenes Roosevelt faced a difficult barrier
to his nomination. Many of the state political machines
were still committed to Al Smith, and any hope for Roosevelt's nomination hinged on his ability to pry loose those
states that wanted Smith to run again in 1932. Unfor-
tunately for Roosevelt, only six other Democratic governors attended the 1930 conference, which gave him
little opportunity to sound out his colleagues at the meeting. But in journeying to Salt Lake City, Roosevelt drew
the attention of a number of pro-Smith western state
parties which eventually turned their support to him.

Summarizing Roosevelt's activities at the 1930 conference, W. A. Warn thought that Roosevelt returned to
New York "written down, not by anything that he said
or did, but through occult mental processes of politicians
who attended that conclave, as a lively and hopeful aspir-
ant for the Democratic nomination. . . ." [5]

The Roosevelt boom spread rapidly as election year
drew nearer. At the 1931 conference, Roosevelt caused
an uproar—and a consequent spate of publicity—when
he departed from the letter of his assigned topic to discuss controversial issues of national agricultural planning.
Since the meeting was at French Lick, Indiana, in the

[4] *New York Times,* July 1, 1930.
[5] *Ibid.,* July 6, 1930.

heart of midwestern farming country, Roosevelt's choice of a provocative agricultural topic was particularly timely. One correspondent caught the political significance of Roosevelt's subject when he said, "To Governor Roosevelt the conference was an opportunity to show the Middle West that he had given thought to the farm problem and that his vision extended beyond the limits of Manhattan." [6]

Roosevelt became an announced candidate early in 1932, which made his appearance at the next Governors' Conference the object of widespread comment in the press. In a speech outside the formal program of the conference, Roosevelt held the spotlight with an oration on George Washington in which he called upon his listeners to learn from Washington "that theory without practical action moves a nation but a short distance along the path of progress. . . . Washington would have us test his policies by present needs, not by blind and unreasoning devotion to mere tradition. . . ." [7]

The forces that eventually led to F.D.R.'s nomination and election were intricate and varied. Certainly the national publicity he received at the Governors' Conference represented only a fraction of the total effort required to place him in the White House. Yet in the eyes of political reporters who covered the pre-convention period, the annual conferences crystallized sentiment about the chances of the ambitious Democratic Governor of New York.

[6] *Ibid.*, June 7, 1931.
[7] *Ibid.*, April 28, 1932.

𝒟 Candidate Dewey

Three elections later, Roosevelt's adversary, Governor Thomas E. Dewey, also took advantage of the conference to boost his standing as a presidential contender. At the Columbus, Ohio, meeting in 1943, Dewey made a major speech on the problem of farm labor. Unlike Roosevelt, Dewey did not use his midwestern setting to court political support in the area. Instead, he openly criticized midwestern corn producers for the shortage of livestock feed then prevailing in the eastern states, and at the same time harshly upbraided the national government's crop restriction policies. At Hershey, Pennsylvania, in 1944, Dewey took on a broader topic. In a survey of the unity of the nation in war and peace, he called for a new responsibility on the part of the states in the postwar years.

More importantly, Dewey relied on the conference as a place for negotiation and talk with his Republican colleagues. Few presidential candidates worked as assiduously with state governors as Dewey did in his futile attempt to unseat Franklin Roosevelt. Behind the closed doors of hotel rooms, Dewey planned with his supporters and labored with the governors who had not yet given him their support.

The results of Dewey's work with the governors showed up most clearly outside the regular meetings of the conference. In 1943, the Republican party assembled a meeting of Republican congressmen, senators, and governors at Mackinac Island, Michigan, to consider the problems of postwar politics and policies. Many of the governors were internationalist in outlook and pro-Dewey in their politics. At the meeting, the Republican governors assailed the isolationists of their party in Congress. The final declaration of the meeting contained a foreign policy plank that was virtually dictated by the internationalist governors. It pledged the party to co-operation in international security measures at the end of the war, including, if necessary, the use of military force.

Dewey then carried the Chicago Republican convention without serious opposition. Almost immediately after his nomination he announced that he was asking all Republican governors to attend a special meeting in St. Louis on August 2-3, 1944. Ostensibly, the purpose of the governors' session was to deal with the question of domestic policies. "We conceive it to be our first obligation," said Dewey, "to bring agreement out of this chaos and to bring unity where there is only disunity now." [8]

The Republican meeting produced outspoken statements on domestic policy, ranging from postwar reconversion to water resources. In general, the policy statements called for federal-state co-operation instead of a hard and fast separation of state and national responsibilities. To bolster the position of the state chief executives, the Republican declaration advocated increased personal contact between the president and governors. Dewey indirectly pledged to work closely with the governors if he were elected.

The St. Louis conference was significant in Dewey's campaign in at least three ways. It enabled the Republican governors to write what was virtually a post-convention party platform. The conference also sharpened the political issues between the Republican and Democratic

[8] *Ibid.*, July 28, 1944.

parties in a manner that the Republican convention, divided as it was between intractable factions, was incapable of doing. Finally, the meeting gave Dewey an opportunity to shore up vitally needed support among the governors who led political organizations in crucial states.

Dewey's loss to Roosevelt in 1944 did not dissuade him from keeping up strong contacts with his fellow governors in the interim between elections. Three years later, Dewey still commanded the support of most Republican governors. In a secret poll conducted at the Salt Lake City Governors' Conference in 1947, ten Republican governors listed Dewey as their first choice for the 1948 nomination, while two governors listed Warren and a few mentioned other candidates or declined to state a preference.[9] En route to the 1947 conference, Dewey followed the precedent of Roosevelt and mended fences with political leaders in several of the western states. At the conference his political fortunes were further enhanced by the refusal of Governor Earl Warren, a leading but unannounced contender for the presidential nomination, to speak out actively as a candidate.

The New York governor's pre-convention campaign reached its peak at the 1948 Governors' Conference, which convened only a week before the Republican convention. Upon his arrival at the New Hampshire conference, Dewey told reporters that he believed his chances for the nomination were "excellent." The statements of other Republican governors confirmed Dewey's predictions, for while several of the state executives supported other candidates, the opposition was sufficiently scattered to give Dewey the dominant share of Republican gubernatorial

[9] *Ibid.,* July 16, 1947.

support. Not long thereafter, the Republican convention selected Dewey as their nominee for the second time—the first occasion on which the Republicans had chosen a once-defeated candidate for a second try.

A Miscellany of Hopefuls

Roosevelt and Dewey managed to derive maximum political benefit from the Governors' Conference in their quest of the presidential nomination. Other governors who became presidential nominees did not take similar advantage of the conference to further their political aims. Coolidge did not attend the Governors' Conference of 1919, and by the time he joined the governors at the December, 1920, meeting, he was already Vice-President-elect.

Governor James M. Cox, of Ohio, the Democratic standard-bearer in 1920, did not bother to attend a single Governors' Conference during his incumbency in 1913–1915 and 1917–1921. Al Smith won the Democratic nomination in 1928 without being present at a Governors' Conference after 1923. Governor Alf Landon, of Kansas, became a member of the conference executive committee in 1935, but there is no evidence that his appearance at the Governors' Conference furthered his Republican nomination in 1936.

Although Governor Adlai Stevenson was a hard-working member of the Governors' Conference, he did not receive widespread notice by the press at the conference until the 1952 meeting. The 1952 conference was held shortly before the Democratic convention. At that late date, Stevenson still declined to announce his candidacy

for the Democratic nomination. He told a press conference that he would consider accepting a genuine draft by
the convention, but would go no further in his statement.
Thus, while he "edged very close to the category of out-
right availability," as the *New York Times* interpreted
his remarks, he still made no public pronouncement of
his presidential aspirations.[10] Behind the scenes, meanwhile, Stevenson supporters were working hard on behalf
of the Illinois governor, and the Democratic convention
eventually picked him as the man to lead their party ticket.

Albert C. Ritchie, of Maryland, and Gifford Pinchot,
of Pennsylvania, both maneuvered at the Governors' Conferences to seek support for their presidential ambitions.
Neither was successful. Most recently, Governor Nelson
Rockefeller, of New York, caused extensive speculation
by his statements at Governors' Conferences. The San
Juan governors' session in 1959 was Rockefeller's first
formal appearance outside the state of New York as governor, and the press was primed to interpret every move
he made as an indication that he was an active candidate
for the Republican nomination in 1960. Rockefeller did
not disappoint the press or his fellow governors. With
impressive speeches in the official part of the conference
and provocative comments at his overflowing press conferences, Rockefeller convinced most of the reporters and
governors that he was seeking the nomination. Yet Rockefeller refused to make any formal announcement of his
candidacy. Later, when it became more apparent that
Vice-President Richard Nixon was far ahead in the race
for convention votes, Rockefeller reversed his field and
ruled himself out of the 1960 presidential contest.

[10] *Ibid.*, July 1, 1952.

The Kingmakers

The governors at the conference have not invariably thumped for their own cause in presidential politics. Some have acted with considerable effectiveness as the emissaries of other presidential prospects. A prime illustration is found in the campaign of 1952, when a group of Republican governors promoted the Eisenhower candidacy. "I have always believed," wrote Edward T. Folliard, "that the Eisenhower-for-President campaign really got off the ground at the Governors' Conference meeting in Gatlinburg, Tenn., in 1951." [11]

A Governors' Conference was an unlikely place to initiate the campaign for a military hero who had not even announced whether he was a Republican or a Democrat, much less that he was interested in running for President. Yet seven Republican governors at the Gatlinburg meeting confidently announced their support for General Eisenhower. Governor Sherman Adams, of New Hampshire, told a press conference that Eisenhower would run and would win, in the New Hampshire primary the following spring. Thomas Dewey; Val Peterson, of Nebraska; Walter J. Kohler, Jr., of Wisconsin; Dan Thornton, of Colorado; Arthur B. Langlie, of Washington; and Edward F. Arn, of Kansas, joined Adams in his support for Eisenhower as the next Republican presidential candidate. "The list of state chief executives who appeared to be in Ike's corner at this time began to suggest an impressive beachhead of organizational support." [12]

[11] *State Government*, Vol. XXXI (Summer, 1958), p. 176.
[12] Paul T. David, Malcolm Moos, and Ralph M. Goldman, *Presidential*

The Eisenhower candidacy moved ahead swiftly. His impressive victory in the New Hampshire primary drew additional support from many Republican quarters, until by the time of the convention the General was a leading contender for the nomination. At that point the Republican governors played another decisive hand.

Before the formal opening of the Republican convention, the national committee was engaged in a critical struggle over the seating of contested delegations from Georgia, Louisiana, and Texas. Some were pledged to Taft, others to Eisenhower. The national committee, leaning toward Senator Taft, proposed to seat fifty Taft delegates and only eleven Eisenhower delegates from the disputed delegations.

While the controversial delegation issue was awaiting action by the full convention, the 1952 Governors' Conference was in session in Houston. Under the leadership of Dewey, the twenty-three Republican governors who were present at the meeting prepared a manifesto concerning the contested delegations. The governors urged that the disputed delegations should not be permitted to vote in the convention until the seating contests had been settled by the remainder of the convention. In effect, this would deny Taft a number of needed votes in the seating disputes. More importantly, the manifesto created an impression that the Taft forces were playing dirty politics in their attempt to seat their delegations. The manifesto was "an obvious shock to the Taft leaders and to the officers of the national committee." [13]

Nominating Politics in 1952, The National Story, Vol. 1 (Baltimore: The Johns Hopkins Press, 1954), p. 27.

[13] *Ibid.,* p. 71. Later, Governor J. Bracken Lee repudiated his support of the Governors' Manifesto.

The governors' suggestion ultimately led to the adoption of a "fair play" resolution which, in amended form, prevented the disputed delegations from voting until their cases had been formally settled by the convention. Under the revised rules, the convention seated the delegations favorable to Eisenhower, greatly boosting the General's convention strength. In retrospect, it appeared that the governors' manifesto "may well have been decisive in enabling the Eisenhower forces to unhinge the desperate drive of the Taft leaders to win the 1952 nomination." [14]

[14] Malcolm Moos, "New Light on the Nominating Process," in Stephen K. Bailey, et al., *Research Frontiers in Politics and Government*, Brookings Lectures, 1955 (Washington: The Brookings Institution, 1955), p. 154.

8

An Omen in the Capital

THE PRESIDENTIAL campaign of 1960 revealed an ominous fact for the American governors. For the second time in history a senator was elected president. For the first time since 1908, no governor ran as a candidate for president or vice-president on a major party ticket. With the single exception of Nelson Rockefeller, no governor of either party received serious consideration for the 1960 nominations.

For some observers the conspicuous absence of the governors was not at all surprising. Rather, it was the natural culmination of a gradual centralization of American politics which gave more and more advantage to leaders in Washington. Thus James Reston detected "a shift . . . in the type of candidate from the solid administrative characters in the State Governors' mansions to the men trained in world and national affairs in Washington, most of them in the Senate." And Arthur Krock, assessing the shift, called it "a fundamental change in American politics."[1]

There is little doubt that profound new forces are reshaping the traditional political pattern. The governors,

[1] *New York Times*, July 10, 1960 (Reston) and June 21, 1960 (Krock).

144

despite their recent ascent into national affairs, face a grave problem of keeping pace with presidential front runners in Washington. For the present, only their position as presidential candidates is threatened. But it is entirely conceivable that the swift changes in political practice could ultimately crack the strongest bastion of the governors—their leadership of state party organizations.

The centralization of politics can be seen in several ways. Voting behavior has become more homogeneous throughout the nation. Geographical regions and ethnic backgrounds formerly were of crucial importance in determining how a person would vote. But present indications are that these factors have become less important. In their place, social class, occupation, and income bracket have emerged as the dividing lines for the voters. Studies of urban voting, for example, showed that Eisenhower in 1952 received about the same proportion of middle-class urban votes in the South as he did in the rest of the country.[2]

Two products of modern technology—television and the jet airplane—have also contributed to the centralization of politics. Estimates of the size of the audience for the first Kennedy-Nixon television debate in 1960 ranged as high as seventy-five million people, with a total audience of over one-hundred million for all of the debates. Purchased television time saps a monumental share of the campaign budgets of both parties.

Television did not, as some predicted, destroy the old whistle-stop campaign. The presidential wars of 1960 were

[2] For a discussion of homogeneity in voting, see Seymour M. Lipset, *Political Man: The Social Bases of Politics* (Garden City, N.Y.: Doubleday and Co., 1960).

fought on more local stumps than any other in history, with both candidates going into nearly every state. Without fast air transportation the task would have been impossible.

Yet modern presidential aspirants have discovered that television appearances and speedy jet hops during the post-convention campaigns are not enough to win elections. Many politicians have concluded that to be serious contenders they need sustained publicity in the national mass media, not simply for the few months between nomination and election, but for two or more years before the conventions. And such publicity might only be achieved by someone—perhaps a senator or a vice-president—who could command almost daily headlines in the national press and nightly close-ups on television newscasts for several years. The presidential election of 1960 was a case in which the nominees had been running hard throughout the country for at least four years.

Under such conditions, politicians are under heavy pressure to nominate nationally popular personalities. The reason is simply that the popular candidate has the best chance of outgunning his competitor. As Roosevelt said, "the first duty of a statesman is to get elected."

Not long ago Professor William G. Carleton contended, in effect, that national party conventions were becoming as vestigial as the electoral college. In his view the processes of mass democracy were turning the conventions into rubber-stamp institutions whose only functions were to ratify the candidacy of the leading favorite in the opinion polls, to endorse predigested platforms written in response to group pressures, and to rally their followers with television spectaculars. This revolution, he said, was

N.B.

affecting the nature of political leadership. "We are approaching a condition where celebrities outside of politics," he said, ". . . carry greater weight in political campaigns than do long-time congressional leaders or state governors." [3]

The Old Advantages

In days gone by, the governors had a convincing set of credentials as presidential aspirants. The governor of New York, California, or Ohio was—and still is—the chief executive of a government larger than many independent nations. Such executive experience was a compelling qualification. Walter Lippman states the case this way:

> It is no accident that since the Nineteenth Century, when the office of President has become so much bigger than it used to be, the successful Presidents have been, with perhaps one exception, men who had learned the art as Governors of states. Whether one likes them or not, the successful Presidents in this century have been Theodore Roosevelt, Woodrow Wilson, Franklin D. Roosevelt, and Harry S. Truman. All but Truman had been Governors. Truman, moreover, was the only President, assuming he was a successful President, who came out of Congress. This is not because Congress is a bad institution but because the work of Congress is very different from that of the Executive. No rule of thumb is absolute. But for my own part there is a reasonable presumption of doubt about the executive competence of any candidate who has never occupied an executive office, as Governor of a state, as Mayor of a big city, or as a Cabinet officer. [4]

[3] William G. Carleton, "The Revolution in the Presidential Nominating Convention," *Political Science Quarterly*, Vol. LXXII (June, 1957), p. 233.
[4] *Washington Post and Times Herald*, March 1, 1960. Similarly, Arthur M. Schlesinger conducted an informal poll of historians and political scientists

A pragmatic argument for the governors was that they were not committed on controversial national issues, while senators and congressmen were subjected to the exposure of roll-call votes. Professional politicians have preferred to choose a candidate who could—at least during the campaign months—be all things to all men.

Governors have customarily claimed more grass-roots support than other presidential candidates. They have preserved the image that they are the officials "closest to the people," and are thus in a good position to gauge public opinion. By inference, a governor close to the people would make a president who would be close to the people, which, in less flattering terms, means that he could be re-elected. This argument has been attenuated in recent years by demonstrations that the national government is often more responsive to grass-roots democratic opinion than state governments.

If other arguments failed, however, the governors could always point to their practically invulnerable status as state party leaders. The nomination of the governor of a large, hotly contested, two party state might guarantee that his own state and region would be won, carrying with them a national electoral majority. This was particularly true for the party out of power, in which the governor of a key state has been a convenient rallying point for party loyalties.

---

to determine scholarly opinion on the stature of American presidents. The poll placed most of the former-governor presidents in the great or near-great category, with a smattering in the average and below-average brackets and none among the failures. Of the presidents selected by national party conventions, the poll listed three great presidents: Governors Wilson and Franklin Roosevelt and Congressman Abraham Lincoln. Arthur M. Schlesinger, "The U.S. Presidents," *Life*, November 1, 1948, pp. 65–66, 68, 73–74.

Strengthened by these advantages and backed by un-wavering party supporters, the governors were in a com-manding position in the nominating conventions. Schol-ars at the Brookings Institution concluded in a major study of the convention process that "The role of the governors as state party leaders and delegation chairmen is one that seems to have taken on increasing importance in recent years." In 1848, not a single governor served as a delegate to the major party conventions. Sixty years later, in 1908, 55 per cent of the Democratic governors and 34 per cent of the Republican governors attended their conventions as delegates. In 1956, 64 per cent of the Democratic governors and 71 per cent of the Republicans were present as delegates. Moreover, the Brookings study indicates that "In recent conventions, if a governor served as a delegate at all, he has been chosen delegation chair-man in about three cases out of four." [5] If a governor is not present at the national convention he may still have active control over his state delegation. In 1952 the Arkan-sas Democratic contingent waited for word from the gover-nor in Little Rock, who kept in communication with political forces at the convention from his office.

The Senators

United States senators have been the most persistent adversaries of governors in the struggle for party leader-ship, but as candidates or as delegation leaders in the con-vention they have seldom been able to best the state ex-ecutives. As one former governor remarked in an inter-

[5] Paul T. David, Ralph M. Goldman, and Richard C. Bain, *The Politics of National Party Conventions* (Washington: The Brookings Institution, 1960), pp. 97–98.

view, "I determined whether or not our senators even attended the convention." David, Goldman, and Bain comment that:

> whereas before 1892 the governors seeking presidential nomination were only about one third as numerous as the senators, since that time the numbers have been about equal. Eight times as many governors as senators, however, have actually been nominated for the Presidency.[6]

Before Kennedy, the only incumbent senator to receive a presidential nomination was Warren G. Harding. His nomination was the special result of a deadlocked convention in which a Republican senatorial faction was able to dictate the eventual selection of their colleague. At the time it seemed that the Republican senators were in firm control of their party. After the nomination of Harding, Governor Livingston Beeckman, of Rhode Island, asked some newspapermen "whether this was a Republican Convention or just a Senatorial caucus."[7]

The triumph of the Republican senators was short lived. Malcolm Moos has observed that "Since 1936, the influence of the congressional element in the latent days of nominating campaigns, as well as in the convention itself, has been relatively minor."[8] A *New York Times* dispatch in 1954 stated that:

> The "old guard" has been the dominant force in Congress and on the national committee in every year since 1936. But it has been unable during all those years—even without a Republican President in the White House—to con-

[6] *Ibid.,* p. 97.

[7] Quoted in Wilfred E. Binkley, *American Political Parties: Their Natural History,* (2nd ed.; New York: Alfred A. Knopf, 1956), p. 348.

[8] In Stephen K. Bailey, *et al, op. cit.,* p. 152.

trol and dominate the national conventions that picked the presidential nominees of 1940, 1944, 1948, and 1952.[9]

Overriding the influence of the senatorial bloc was a forceful group of Republican governors led by such men as Dewey of New York, Warren of California, Youngdahl of Minnesota, Driscoll of New Jersey, Herter of Massachusetts, and Adams of New Hampshire. While they did not hold all power within the Republican ranks, their personal leadership went far in the remolding of the party that captured the presidency in 1952.

The Case of Kennedy

It could not last forever. Months before the 1960 conventions assembled, Pollster Louis Harris published an article which listed "some of the underlying reasons Governors seem to be fading as ideal Presidential candidates in general, and in 1960 in particular."

Presidential candidates, he noted, need a long spell of national publicity, but governors "have shrunk to being thought of all too often as local figures." The increasing importance of national and world affairs greatly aided the senators and other national figures, while the governors, he said, "lack a foreign affairs dimension." Moreover, senators have a "mobility and a far-reaching range that has been difficult for any Governor to match."

Even more significantly, Harris observed that the state governors were in dangerous political trouble in their home states. The pressure for new state services put the governors into painful revenue predicaments, and their

---

[9] *New York Times*, December 19, 1954.

popularity at home tended to plummet with every new tax bill. Governors were having so much trouble staying alive politically that they scarcely had time to think of running for national office.

Granting that governors still maintained leadership in their state party organizations, Harris concluded that "for the moment at least, and perhaps for some years into the future, the road to the White House from a governorship will be a lot longer and rougher than it has been in the past." [10]

The 1960 elections seemed to confirm that the governors were in difficulty. The nomination of Kennedy, Johnson, Nixon, and Lodge left the aspiring governors at the starting gate. In the states, many governors had serious trouble. Republican candidates for governor were defeated in heavily Republican North Dakota, Nebraska, and Indiana. Democrats lost the statehouses in Massachusetts, New Mexico, and Minnesota, which voted for Kennedy.

Both Kennedy and Nixon fitted the particulars of the new type of presidential candidate. They had made their reputations in Washington and had built them steadily over a period of years. They had little executive experience to offer, but both accented their widespread knowledge of national and world affairs. Kennedy used his high standings in the opinion polls as a lever to pry support from recalcitrant party leaders, while Nixon placed heavy reliance on his national prestige as Vice-President. Both had a touch of glamour. The candidates' wives and famous friends were frequently mentioned in campaign propa-

[10] Louis Harris, "Why the Odds Are Against a Governor's Becoming President," *Public Opinion Quarterly*, Vol. XXIII (Fall, 1959), pp. 361–70.

ganda. And in keeping with a growing political practice, Hollywood threw its stars and celebrities into the struggle.

At first blush, then, it appeared that the political revolution was complete, with popular national figures in firm control. On closer examination, however, the revolution is not nearly as thoroughgoing as some might hasten to conclude. Nor is the threat to the governors as fatal as it seemed in the turbulence of the early sixties.

The voting pattern of the 1960 presidential election, for example, was not as homogeneous as voting analysts had anticipated. To be sure, social class, occupation, and income were crucial determinants, but many of the old factors re-entered the pattern. Regionalism, which had once been highly significant, returned with all engines going. The eastern seaboard voted heavily Democratic, while the western states supported Nixon overwhelmingly. The vote in the South, while no longer solid, was nevertheless strongly conditioned by the presence of a southerner on the Democratic ticket. And the midwestern farmers still voted as a discernible bloc.

Religion was thought to be secondary in contemporary voting, but the presence of a Roman Catholic on the ticket influenced the choice of both Protestants and Catholics with decisive results. Negroes again voted as a solid racial bloc for the Democratic party, reversing their gradual movement toward the Republicans. In short, politicians could not rely on uniform political pitches based only on social class or occupation; the old complicated pattern of American politics was still very much alive.

Some observers thought that old-style political organization was becoming outdated in the age of television politics. The 1960 elections proved rather conclusively that professional politicians played a crucial role in the election. Political organizations in New York City, Philadelphia, Chicago, and Baltimore, to mention only a few, delivered votes that helped to give the victory to John Kennedy. The Republican organizations were functioning, too, but without the same effectiveness.

Another fact is of particular importance in assessing the present status of the governors in national politics. In the Democratic party, state governors were the pivotal figures in the 1960 presidential campaign. It is helpful at this point to review the part taken by the governors in Kennedy's final victory.[11]

The Governors and Kennedy

Although the Kennedy campaign for the nomination had been underway since the 1956 Democratic convention, it remained *sub rosa* until the last few months of work. But a full year before the Democrats selected Senator Kennedy, Governor Foster Furcolo, of Massachusetts, and Governor Abraham Ribicoff, of Connecticut, were laboring among their colleagues at the 1959 Governors' Conference on behalf of Kennedy. The governors also seized every opportunity to spread the Kennedy name before the large press corps present at the conference. They continued their work in the remaining months, and were still putting finishing touches on the Kennedy band wagon at the 1960 Governors' Conference.

An early break-through for Kennedy came in Ohio when Governor Michael V. DiSalle announced in Jan-

[11] The following information is based in part on letters received from twenty-six Democratic governors or their secretaries after the Kennedy nomination.

uary that he would take to the Democratic convention a favorite son delegation pledged to vote for John Kennedy. Columnist Marquis Childs promptly spotted the move as "a tremendous spur" to the Kennedy organization,[12] and Governor DiSalle pointed out later that "many people say that the turning point in Senator Kennedy's campaign was . . . when Ohio announced its position." The Ohio Governor added that "Although neither Senator from Ohio was particularly in sympathy with this move, there was no effort on their part to contest the decision." [13]

The Kennedy campaign continued to pick up steam in the Wisconsin and West Virginia primaries, and then settled into the long summer stretch until convention time. During that period, Michigan's Governor G. Mennen Williams gave a helpful assist to the Kennedy cause when he announced his support for the Senator on June 2. "My motive on this timing," said the Governor, "was a judgment that Senator Kennedy's campaign needed a new push to help it continue the momentum of the primaries." [14]

With Kennedy clearly the front runner in the Democratic ranks, one by one other governors threw their personal support and their organizations behind the senator. As the convention assembled, Kennedy endorsements

---

[12] *Washington Post and Times Herald,* January 15, 1960.

[13] Letter to the author, August 2, 1960. Governor DiSalle also noted, in comparing the political strength of governors and senators, that "In many states where there were Democratic senators, they were not able to do much on behalf of their preferred candidate. For example, Senator Thomas Dodd of Connecticut was strongly for Johnson but could not even cast his own vote since Connecticut was bound by the unit rule. Senator McCarthy of Minnesota was strongly for Governor Stevenson but was not able to cast his vote because Minnesota was bound to Senator Humphrey. In Montana both Senators were supporting Senator Johnson but Montana cast a majority for Senator Kennedy."

[14] Letter to the author, August 8, 1960.

came from Brown of California, McNichols of Colorado, Loveless of Iowa, Docking of Kansas, Freeman of Minnesota, Sawyer of Nevada, Edmondson of Oklahoma, the all-important Lawrence of Pennsylvania, Rosellini of Washington, and Nelson of Wisconsin. Most of the Democratic governors were chairmen of their state delegations, and an endorsement of Kennedy meant part if not all of their states' support.[15] Other governors would have thrown their delegation's votes to Kennedy on the second ballot if a first ballot triumph had not occurred.

After their return from the Governors' Conference in late June, many of the governors were convinced that Kennedy would receive the nomination. Massachusetts Governor Furcolo's office reported in retrospect that their tally of delegate votes at the Governors' Conference "coincided almost exactly with what the ultimate outcome of the Convention revealed." [16]

If the governors' support of Kennedy during the preconvention campaign was helpful, their support during the drive to election was critical. A number of southern governors had initially supported Senator Lyndon Johnson and were sitting on their hands after the convention. Senator Johnson, as Kennedy's emissary, convinced these governors that they should go into action on behalf of the Democratic ticket, and it may be that the organizational support for the Kennedy-Johnson ticket in the South was the needed push to carry many of the southern states. In important states throughout the country, Democratic governors hurled their organizations into action. When the election dust settled and Senator Kennedy

[15] An exception was Oklahoma, which voted for Johnson.
[16] Letter to the author, September 13, 1960.

turned to the job of selecting his cabinet, the names of governors once more sprang into prominence. Three incumbent governors—Ribicoff, Hodges, and Freeman—were made cabinet members, while Mennen Williams took a major State Department post and several former governors, including Stevenson and Bowles, accepted key positions in the new administration. In striking contrast, United States Senators—those with whom Kennedy had worked most closely—were not asked to assume large responsibilities in the executive branch.

Governors and Future Elections

The election of Kennedy was a case in which the governors decided to support a popular national figure rather than one of their own kind. The Republican governors did the same when they supported Eisenhower in 1952. Their action indicates that the governors have had to roll with the punch of national publicity and popularity, and it genuinely signals that new hazards lie ahead for the governors. The political future of the governors will be seriously jeopardized unless they readjust their partisan weaponry to meet the new challenge of television politics and the growing importance of international events.

But there are signs that the governors have the ability to adapt to their new environment. Rockefeller, for example, is in a considerably stronger position as governor of New York than he would have been as senator from the same state. In any event, governors can win presidential nominations in the future, although it will not be for the same old reasons. They will, of course, offer administrative experience as an asset, but the modern president is first a policy-maker and secondarily an administrator. If governors in the past were chosen because they were politically uncommitted on vital issues, the modern governor is much more likely to make his position known on national problems while he is still in the statehouse. The national policy stands of Nelson Rockefeller were more explicit than the stands of Richard Nixon.

Modern presidential nominees require a long build-up in advance, and the governor who wants the nomination will not be able, as he was in the past, to sit on the side lines until the last minute before the convention. He must start his campaigns early and keep his name before the public. This places the governors of the small states at a disadvantage, but then they have never enjoyed much favor as nominees. Instead, the parties have turned to governors of the largest states for their candidates. The governors of these states have massive resources for publicity and are prepared to use them in competition with senators and other hopefuls.

Even long range publicity may be inadequate. It is possible that John Kennedy, after campaigning for four years, was still not sufficiently known to win an election at the time of his nomination. The memorable television debates with the better-known Nixon afforded the chance for a final burst of national publicity. By the same token, a popular governor with good advance publicity could be catapulted to presidential victory in crucial television appearances.

The governors themselves have few doubts about their influence in national party politics. Former Governor Robert F. Kennon, of Louisiana, flatly asserted in an interview that "governors control their parties and they control the presidential nominations." [17]

In the judgment of Illinois' William Stratton, the centralization of American politics, if such were actually happening, would have little effect on the political position of the governors. Noting that the Republican governors stopped Senator Taft and made possible the nomination of General Eisenhower, Stratton said:

> There's a big difference between political effectiveness and political notoriety. The fact that a governor isn't seen at a Washington cocktail party doesn't mean he isn't a formidable contender. You still have to get elected at home. And governors generally control party politics in the states.[18]

"The myths against the political acceptability of senators has been removed, I hope forever," said Governor Mennen Williams, "but this does not mean that governors now go into eclipse." [19] It remains to be seen.

[17] Interview, May 15, 1959
[18] Interview, June 9, 1959.
[19] Letter to the author, August 8, 1960.

9

The Governors at
Mid-Century

TRADITIONALLY the national and state levels of American government have been viewed as distinctly separate parts of the federal system, even though it has long been obvious that they overlap and commingle to a large degree. Ever since the New Deal, the political structure has been revolutionized by intertwining relationships between the states and the nation. Instead of maintaining a rigid separation of responsibilities, the different levels now share many functions and tax sources.

It is indeed an era of co-operative federalism. As Professor Morton Grodzins has more vividly expressed it, the old image of the federal system as a layer cake, with neat distinctions between each level of government, is no longer valid; today with its highly diffused responsibilities the system more nearly resembles a marble cake in which national and state functions have been swirled together. The change to a marble cake federalism, moreover, is likely to be permanent. At least, as Roscoe Drummond once said, it would be as hard to restore the old federalism as it would be to put the apple pie back in the apple

The New American Governor

The conception of a rigid separation between governments still persists and distorts the image of the role that
officials now play within the political system. Upon close
examination, it is now clear that the responsibilities of
state governors have significantly changed under the pressures of co-operative federalism. The governor of fifty
years ago was preoccupied with the internal business of
the state without reference to national problems. Since
that time, the interests of the national government have
been fused with the interests of the states so much that a
governor spends a large portion of his working day with
national affairs. State constitutions make no reference to
these national interests, but it is apparent that the governors are active participants in the fortunes of the national government.

Former Governor Herschel Loveless, of Iowa, once esti-
mated that he spent from eight to ten hours a week on
questions of national policy, while Missouri's former Governor James Blair, Jr. thought that national problems
must take at least 20 per cent of the time of an average
governor.[1] Aside from national business at home, most
governors make several trips to Washington each year to
testify before congressional committees, to take care of
business in the executive departments, or to participate
in national party affairs.

The key point is that a modern governor cannot always
separate national issues from state issues. He deals with
problems of public policy which may simultaneously in-

[1] Interviews, August 4, 1959.

volve the interests of local, state, and national governments. In so doing, the governor must be re-defined as a new kind of political executive. He is no longer simply the chief executive of the internal business of his state. He is a factor in the federal system as a whole, a link and a pivot in the diffused relationship of the states and the national government.

The existing literature on the American state governors does not reflect this involvement of the governor in national affairs. Most studies, following traditional constitutional definitions of the governorship, are strictly confined to intrastate responsibilities of the governors. The result is a consequent distortion of the governor's actual role. This is not to criticize the competent studies that have been made.[2] Insofar as they can be isolated from national matters, internal state affairs continue to dominate a governor's responsibilities. At the same time, a full description of what a governor actually does must incorporate his activities in the national government and give attention to the intermingling of state and national affairs.

The Conference as an Institution

Within the complex federal system the institution of the Governors' Conference occupies a unique position.

---

[2] See Leslie Lipson, *The American Governor from Figurehead to Leader* (Chicago: University of Chicago Press, 1939), which is a survey of the evolution of the governorship. See also Coleman B. Ransone, Jr., *The Office of Governor in the South* (University, Ala.: University of Alabama Bureau of Public Administration, 1951), and *The Office of Governor in the United States* (University, Ala.: University of Alabama Press, 1956). Ransone broke away from a rigid adherence to constitutional definitions of the governorship to analyze the time actually spent by the governors, but he did not attempt to distinguish between internal state responsibilities and national responsibilities.

While it is not a formal part of the governmental system, the fact that its members are public officials rather than private citizens gives the conference a special standing in the political life of the nation. The public position of the governors distinguishes the conference from the many private groups which have an important place in the political process. The public office of the governors does not automatically guarantee that the conference will be more influential than private groups. On the contrary, the evidence indicates that the Governors' Conference has at best a modest influence on the development of public policies. Potentially, however, a highly organized group of state governors, each of whom commands powerful political resources, is a formidable contender in the game of politics.

As an institution the conference has developed increasing strength. It is no longer a casual meeting of state chief executives. It is a permanent, extraconstitutional body equipped with its own bureaucracy. It actively seeks to influence national policy in Congress and in the executive branch. The conference has developed formal procedures, extensive committee systems, and a written constitution which is subject to amendment by the constituent body. Hierarchical patterns of leadership have developed within the conference. The chairmanship of the executive committee or even membership in the executive committee is considered a valuable political asset. Each of these developments has contributed to the permanence of the conference as a political institution.

With only fifty-odd years of political life behind it, however, the Governors' Conference cannot claim to be a mighty force in public policy formation. The governors themselves view the effectiveness of the conference with appropriate reserve. A former conference chairman, Governor William P. Lane, Jr., believes that the greatest value of the conference lies in its ability to moderate the provincial outlook of the governors. Given the opportunity to compare notes on problems, the governors "become a little bit more human," he said.[3]

Another former chairman, Robert F. Kennon, observed that the individualism of the state executives placed inherent limitations on the collective authority of the conference. "The Governors' Conference," he said, "won't be a major national force. Governors run their own shops and they won't be run by an association. They won't be bound, caucus-style, and any such move would destroy its most valuable function, which is the exchange of information."[4]

Governor William Stratton assigned three principal functions to the conference. It is, he said, a means of knowing other governors and working together with them; it provides a means for the discussion and solution of technical issues; and it focuses public attention on the role of state government in the federal system.[5] This last point is similar to the view of Thomas Dewey, who remarked that the conference "has been a powerful force for increasing the stature of the states in the federal system."[6]

Perhaps the most balanced summary of the significance of the Governors' Conference was offered by Adlai E. Stevenson, who said:

In a flexible, cooperative federalism there is room, and imperative necessity, for strength at each level of government.

[3] Interview, November 19, 1959.
[4] Interview, May 15, 1959.
[5] Interview, June 9, 1959.
[6] *State Government*, Vol. XXXI (Summer, 1958), p. 169.

The Governors' Conference is serving such a federalism in its search and leadership for more logic and order in federal-state relations; in its opposition to needless transfer of tasks to Washington; in the impetus it gives for interstate cooperation; above all in the studies and leadership through which it seeks to strengthen state government in structure and administration and to make state services more adequate for our times.[7]

As a collective force, then, the Governors' Conference has three functions:

1) The conference enables the governors to apply direct political influence on the national government. Policy resolutions, special committees, and contacts by individual governors have been of considerable importance in the formation of several major national policies. The conference has been a proving ground for intergovernmental arrangements, for it has given governors a chance to compare notes on their experiences with the national government. This comparison of experiences has also reduced extremism among the governors and has encouraged a disciplined, systematic approach to federal problems instead of a noisy but ineffectual hostility.

2) It furnishes a means of studying, discussing, and exchanging information on problems of state government. This study has shown that the governors are decidedly more reluctant to exert any collective pressure on the states than on the national government. Only a small percentage of conference policy resolutions, for example, have been directed to state government. But staff studies and projects have been extremely valuable to the states.

3) The conference gives the governors a nationwide forum for partisan political activity, thereby keeping them in the national eye at a time when mass-media communi-

[7] *Ibid.*, p. 172.

cation gives a great advantage to the politician who commands a national audience.

David, Goldman, and Bain, in their study of the national conventions, have argued that the Governors' Conference should be organized along party lines in order to give governors a better preparation for nomination to national office. They suggest that party national committees could provide staff assistance to the party "caucuses" that occur at the conferences. "Perhaps," they add, "if the realities of the two-party system are to be fully recognized in the governors' conference, the time has even come to abandon the amiable pretense that the sessions . . . are 'nonpolitical.' " [8]

While the governors definitely could use better preparation for national office, as David, Goldman, and Bain suggest, it is doubtful that their plan for a partisan conference would be of much help. In the first place, the nonpolitical atmosphere of the formal sessions is considerably more than "amiable pretense." When governors convene, the things that make them agree as governors are, with a few exceptions, more important than the things that would make them disagree as Republicans and Democrats. When they discuss highway construction, the National Guard, or federal tax policies, they tend to agree on the issues regardless of party affiliation. It would require much more than an "amiable pretense" to get a conservative Republican governor to agree with a liberal Democrat to invite officials of the Soviet Union to the United States. Yet similar events occur at every Governors' Conference.

In the second place, the greatest partisan benefits at the conference appear outside the conference room, where the

[8] Paul T. David, Ralph M. Goldman, and Richard C. Bain, *op. cit.*, p. 487.

governors are free to play party politics with gusto. They can stump for candidates, hold press conferences, and revile or defend the national administration. Meanwhile, there is still serious federal-state business to be done within the regular conference sessions. A conference reorganized along partisan lines could have the slightly ludicrous appearance of a baseball farm team working out in the boondocks, hoping for the chance to get to the major leagues.

The time may come, of course, when most federal-state issues will break along party lines. The governors in 1960 voted for the Democratic old age medical plan tied to Social Security and against Eisenhower's federal-state plan. Six Republican governors supported the Social Security plan; eight opposed it. Twenty-four Democrats voted for it, while four voted against it.[9] While the Republicans divided rather evenly, the Democratic governors heavily opposed the Eisenhower position.

For the present, however, the common interests of the governors are still greater than their differences, and any attempt to force the conference proceedings into a partisan strait jacket could hamper the effectiveness of the conference at all levels of government.

The Counterrevolution in American Federalism

There is an old adage which goes, "if you can't lick 'em, join 'em." It well sums up what the national activity of the governors indicates about the federal system as a whole. The governors have not invariably sought to turn back the

---

[9] One territorial governor supported the Eisenhower plan but expressed no party affiliation.

invading national government at the borders of the states. They have, on the contrary and despite their vocal protests, received many inroads of the national government as part of the natural course of politics. Rather than bluntly attacking the federal revolution by fighting for a return to the old days, the governors have absorbed the thrust of the national government, accepting many of its innovations and its supervision.

Having accepted the national invasion, however, the governors have sought to influence or control the policies of the invader. By accepting the fact of the nationalization of many activities formerly left to the jurisdiction of the states, the governors have bowed to new economic and political forces. At the same time, they have sought to shape the relevant policies of the national government in a manner convenient to the states.

The governors accepted national mastery of the interstate highway program, but were instrumental in writing the 1956 federal highway bill. They worked hard for improved civil defense measures controlled by the national government, but asked a major voice in the development of the federal program. The governors welcomed national participation in airport construction, insisting at the same time on their right to manage negotiations within the states. They did not argue that the financing and control of public assistance should be handed to the states; they did seek an effective public assistance program operated jointly by the states and the national government. The governors have not challenged national responsibility for foreign affairs. They have, however, welcomed the opportunity to confer with Soviet and Latin American officials, to make pronouncements on international economics, and to press for United States support for the United Nations, the Marshall Plan, and the North Atlantic Treaty Organization.

On other fronts, the state executives have continued to play their time-honored role as guardians of the states. When the national government hinted at a permanent nationalization of the employment security program, the governors stoutly defended the authority of the states in that field. They have resisted the proliferation of national taxes that threatened to deplete state tax sources. But in general, their greatest objections have concerned procedures rather than the substance of national policies. It is particularly notable that the Governors' Conference objected most forcefully to national intrusions during the administrations of Harding, Coolidge, and Hoover, not during the period since the New Deal.

Despite their devotion to state government—or perhaps because of it—many governors have accepted national participation in state affairs. Politically and administratively many states have been unprepared to handle the demand for new public programs. Hobbled by tax restrictions, party conflict, or special interest groups, nearly all states have encountered a severe crisis in government. In comparison, the national government has been able to assist the states with relative ease.

Thus it has been that the governors, by their willingness to support national policies and to work for their improvement rather than their repeal, have reinforced the current pattern of co-operative federalism. Their attitude presages a creative era in the American political system.

Appendix

THE ANNUAL GOVERNORS' CONFERENCES, 1908–1961

DATE	LOCATION	EXECUTIVE COMMITTEE CHAIRMAN (term beginning at meeting)
1908 May 13–15	Washington, D.C.	*
1910 Jan. 18–20	Washington, D.C.	*
1910 Nov. 29–Dec. 1	Frankfort and Louisville, Ky.	*
1911 Sept. 12–16	Spring Lake, N.J.	Francis E. McGovern, Wis. (R)
1912 Dec. 3–7	Richmond, Va.	Francis E. McGovern, Wis. (R)
1913 Aug. 26–29	Colorado Springs, Colo.	Francis E. McGovern, Wis. (R)
1914 Nov. 10–13	Madison, Wis.	David I. Walsh, Mass. (D)
1915 Aug. 24–27	Boston, Mass.	William Spry, Utah (R)
1916 Dec. 14–16	Washington, D.C.	Arthur Capper, Kansas (R)
1917 ———	No meeting	———
1918 Dec. 16–18	Annapolis, Md.	Emerson C. Harrington, Md. (D) succeeded by Henry J. Allen, Kansas (R)
1919 Aug. 18–21	Salt Lake City, Utah	William C. Sproul, Pa. (R)
1920 Dec. 1–3	Harrisburg, Pa.	William C. Sproul, Pa. (R)
1921 Dec. 5–7	Charleston, S.C.	William C. Sproul, Pa. (R)
1922 Dec. 14–16	White Sulphur Springs, West Va.	Channing H. Cox, Mass. (R)
1923 Oct. 17–19	West Baden, Ind.	Channing H. Cox, Mass. (R)
1924 Nov. 17–18	Jacksonville, Fla.	E. Lee Trinkle, Va. (D)
1925 June 29–July 1	Poland Springs, Maine	Ralph O. Brewster, Maine (R)
1926 July 26–28	Cheyenne, Wyo.	Ralph O. Brewster, Maine (R)
1927 July 25–27	Mackinac Island, Mich.	Adam McMullen, Neb. (R)
1928 Nov. 20–22	New Orleans, La.	George H. Dern, Utah (D)
1929 July 16–18	New London, Conn.	George H. Dern, Utah (D)

* Note: The executive committee was not organized until 1911. At the 1908 meeting President Theodore Roosevelt presided. Governor Augustus E. Willson of Kentucky (R) served as informal conference chairman at the two meetings in 1910.

1930	June 30— July 2	Salt Lake City, Utah	Norman S. Case, R.I. (R)
1931	June 1–2	French Lick, Ind.	Norman S. Case, R.I. (R)
1932	Apr. 25–27	Richmond, Va.	Norman S. Case, R.I. (R) succeeded by John G. Pollard, Va. (D)
1933	July 24–26	Sacramento and San Francisco, Calif.	James Rolph, Jr., Calif. (R)
1934	July 26–27	Mackinac Island, Mich.	Paul V. NcNutt, Ind. (D)
1935	June 13–15	Biloxi, Miss.	Paul V. NcNutt, Ind. (D)
1936	Nov. 16–18	St. Louis, Mo.	George C. Peery, Va. (D)
1937	Sept. 14-16	Atlantic City, N.J.	Robert L. Cochran, Neb. (D)
1938	Sept. 26–28	Oklahoma City, Okla.	Robert L. Cochran, Neb. (D)
1939	June 26–29	Albany and New York City, N.Y.	Lloyd C. Stark, Mo. (D)
1940	June 2–5	Duluth, Minn.	William H. Vanderbilt, R.I. (R)
1941	June 29— July 2	Boston and Cambridge, Mass.	Harold E. Stassen, Minn. (R)
1942	June 21–24	Asheville, N.C.	Herbert R. O'Conor, Md. (D)
1943	June 20–23	Columbus, Ohio	Leverett Saltonstall, Mass. (R)
1944	May 28–31	Hershey, Pa.	Herbert B. Maw, Utah (D)
1945	July 1–4	Mackinac Island, Mich.	Edward Martin, Pa. (R)
1946	May 26–29	Oklahoma City, Okla.	Millard F. Caldwell, Fla. (D)
1947	July 14–16	Salt Lake City, Utah	Horace A. Hildreth, Maine (R)
1948	June 13–16	Portsmouth, N.H.	Lester C. Hunt, Wyo. (D) succeeded by William P. Lane, Jr., Md. (D)
1949	June 19–22	Colorado Springs, Colo.	Frank Carlson, Kansas (R)
1950	June 19–21	White Sulphur Springs, West Va.	Frank J. Lausche, Ohio (D)
1951	Sept. 30— Oct. 3	Gatlinburg, Tenn.	Val Peterson, Neb. (R)
1952	June 29— July 2	Houston, Texas	Allan Shivers, Texas (D)
1953	Aug. 3–6	Seattle, Wash.	Dan Thornton, Colo. (R)
1954	July 11–14	Lake George, N.Y.	Robert F. Kennon, La. (D)
1955	Aug. 9–12	Chicago, Ill.	Arthur B. Langlie, Wash. (R)
1956	June 25–27	Atlantic City, N.J.	Thomas B. Stanley, Va. (D)
1957	June 24–26	Williamsburg, Va.	William G. Stratton, Ill. (R)
1958	May 18–21	Bal Harbour, Fla.	LeRoy Collins, Fla. (D)
1959	Aug. 3–5	San Juan, Puerto Rico	J. Caleb Boggs, Del. (R)
1960	June 26–29	Glacier National Park, Montana	Stephen L. R. McNichols, Colo. (D)
1961	June 25–28	Honolulu, Hawaii	

Bibliography

Books and Reports

Alexander, Margaret C. *The Development of the Power of the State Executive.* Smith College Studies in History, II (April, 1917), pp. 147–233.

Anderson, William. *Federalism and Intergovernmental Relations: A Budget of Suggestions for Research.* Chicago: Public Administration Service, 1946.

———. *The Nation and the States, Rivals or Partners?* Minneapolis: University of Minnesota Press, 1955.

Anderson, William, with the assistance of Durfee, Waite D., Jr., and staff. *Intergovernmental Fiscal Relations.* Research Monograph No. 8, Intergovernmental Relations in the United States as Observed in the State of Minnesota, eds. William Anderson and Edward W. Weidner. Minneapolis: University of Minnesota Press, 1956.

Bellush, Bernard. *Franklin D. Roosevelt as Governor of New York.* New York: Columbia University Press, 1955.

Benson, George C. S. *The New Centralization: A Study of Intergovernmental Relationships in the United States.* New York: Farrar and Rinehart, Inc., 1941.

Blau, Peter M. *Bureaucracy in Modern Society.* New York: Random House, 1956.

Clark, Jane Perry. *The Rise of a New Federalism: Federal-State Cooperation in the United States.* New York: Columbia University Press, 1938.

Congressional Quarterly Almanac, Vols. I–XV (1945 through 1959).

Council of State Governments. *The Book of the States.* Biennial, 1935–1961. Chicago: Council of State Governments.

———. *Federal Grants-in-Aid.* Chicago: Council of State Governments, 1949.

———. *The Governors of the States, 1900–1958.* Chicago: Council of State Governments, 1957.

———. *Reorganizing State Government.* Chicago: Council of State Governments, 1950.

Crennan, Charles Halloway. *A Survey of State Executive Organization and a Plan of Reorganization.* Menasha, Wis.: George Banta Publishing Co., 1916.

David, Paul T., Goldman, Ralph M., and Bain, Richard C. *The Politics of National Party Conventions.* Washington, D.C.: The Brookings Institution, 1960.

David, Paul T., Moos, Malcolm C., and Goldman, Ralph M., (eds.). *Presidential*

Nominating Politics in 1952. 5 Vols. Baltimore: The Johns Hopkins Press, 1954.

Gaus, John M. *Reflections on Public Administration.* University, Ala.: University of Alabama Press, 1947.

Governors' Conference. *Governors of the American States, Commonwealths, and Territories.* Chicago: The Governors' Conference, published annually in recent years as a handbook for the meetings.

————. *Proceedings,* 1908 through 1960. No volume published in 1917.

Graves, W. Brooke (ed.). *Intergovernmental Relations in the United States.* Annals of the American Academy of Political and Social Science, January, 1940.

Greene, Evarts B. *The Provincial Governor in the English Colonies of North America.* New York: Longmans, Green, and Co., 1898.

Hesseltine, William B. *Lincoln and the War Governors.* New York: Alfred A. Knopf, 1948.

Hunter, Floyd. *Top Leadership, U.S.A.* Chapel Hill: University of North Carolina Press, 1959.

Joint Federal-State Action Committee. *Report to the President of the United States and to the Chairman of the Governors' Conference, Progress Report No. 1.* Washington, D.C.: U.S. Government Printing Office, December, 1957.

————. *Progress Report No. 2.* December, 1958.

————. *Final Report.* February, 1960.

Jordan, William George. *The House of Governors: A New Idea in American Politics Aiming to Promote Uniform Legislation on Vital Questions, to Conserve States Rights, to Lessen Centralization, to Secure a Fuller, Freer Voice of the People, and to Make a Stronger Nation.* New York: Jordan Publishing Company, 1907.

Key, V. O., Jr. *The Administration of Federal Grants to States.* Chicago: Public Administration Service, 1937.

————. *American State Politics: An Introduction.* New York: Alfred A. Knopf, 1956.

Lipson, Leslie. *The American Governor from Figurehead to Leader.* Chicago: University of Chicago Press, 1939.

MacDonald, Austin F. *Federal Subsidies to the States: A Study in American Administration.* Philadelphia: University of Pennsylvania, 1923 (printed Ph.D. thesis).

MacMahon, Arthur W. (ed.). *Federalism Mature and Emergent.* Garden City, N.Y.: Doubleday and Co., 1955.

Macmillan, Margaret B. *The War Governors in the American Revolution.* Columbia University Studies in History, Economics, and Public Law No. 503. New York: Columbia University Press, 1943.

Mills, C. Wright. *The Power Elite.* New York: Oxford University Press, 1956.

Moos, Malcolm. *The Republicans: A History of Their Party.* New York: Random House, 1956.

Plumb, Ralph Gordon. *Our American Governors.* Manitowoc [?] Wis., 1956.

Ransone, Coleman B., Jr. *The Office of Governor in the South*. University, Ala. University of Alabama Bureau of Public Administration, 1951.

———. *The Office of Governor in the United States*. University, Ala.: University of Alabama Press, 1956.

Rourke, Francis E. *Intergovernmental Relations in Employment Security*. Research Monograph No. 6, Intergovernmental Relations in the United States as Observed in the State of Minnesota, eds. William Anderson and Edward W. Weidner. Minneapolis: University of Minnesota Press, 1952.

Schlesinger, Joseph A. *How They Became Governor: A Study of Comparative State Politics, 1870–1950*. East Lansing: Governmental Research Bureau, Michigan State University, 1957.

Wheare, K. C. *Federal Government*. 3rd ed. London: Oxford University Press, 1953.

White, Leonard D. *The States and the Nation*. Baton Rouge: Louisiana State University Press, 1953.

Articles

Anderson, William. "Executives: National and State," *Public Administration Review*, Vol. XII (Winter, 1952), pp. 55–59.

"As Newspapermen See the Conference." [Roscoe Drummond, Leo Egan, Edward T. Folliard, and Jack Steele] *State Government*, Vol. XXXI (Summer, 1958), pp. 173–77.

Bane, Frank. "The Citizen Civilian Army," in Leonard D. White, ed., *Civil Service in Wartime*, Charles R. Walgreen Foundation Lectures. Chicago: University of Chicago Press, 1945, pp. 142–59.

———. "The Job of Being a Governor," *State Government*, Vol. XXXI (Summer, 1958), pp. 184–89.

Carleton, William G. "The Revolution in the Presidential Nominating Convention," *Political Science Quarterly*, Vol. LXXII (June, 1957), pp. 224–40.

Collins, LeRoy. "Can a Southerner Be Elected President?" remarks at Southern Governors' Conference, September 23, 1957.

David, Paul T. "The Role of Governors at the National Party Conventions," *State Government*, Vol. XXXIII (Spring, 1960), pp. 103–10.

"Do Governors Meet for Fun?" *State Government*, Vol. IV (June, 1931), pp. 14–15.

Ewing, Cortez A. M. "Southern Governors," *Journal of Politics*, Vol. X (May, 1948), pp. 385–409.

Fairlie, John A. "The State Governor," *Michigan Law Review*, Vol. X (March and April, 1912), pp. 370–83, 458–75.

"Five Former Governors Appraise the Governors' Conference." [Thomas E. Dewey, Frank M. Dixon, Frank J. Lausche, Leverett Saltonstall, and Adlai E. Stevenson] *State Government*, Vol. XXXI (Summer, 1958), pp. 168–72.

Gaus, John M. "The States Are in the Middle," *State Government*, Vol. XXIII (June, 1950), pp. 138–42.

"The Governors at Washington," *The Nation*, Vol. LXXXVI (May 21, 1908), p. 460.

"Governors' Conference 1908-1946." *State Government*, Vol. XIX (July, 1946), pp. 184-89.

Graves, W. Brooke. "What is Happening to Our Federal System?" *State Government*, Vol. XXII (November, 1949), pp. 255-59, 270.

Gravlin, Leslie M. "An Effective Chief Executive," *National Municipal Review*, Vol. XXXVI (March, 1947), pp. 137-41.

Greenberg, Betty. "The Governors' Conference and Federal-State Relations." Unpublished mss., Council of State Governments, typed.

Grodzins, Morton. "American Political Parties and the American System." Unpublished mss., mimeo., c. 1959.

"Growth of Cooperative Government." *State Government*, Vol. XVII (January, 1944), pp. 26-63, 268.

Harris, Joseph P. "The Governors' Conference: Retrospect and Prospect," *State Government*, Vol. XXXI (Summer, 1958), pp. 190-96.

Harris, Louis. "Why the Odds Are Against a Governor's Becoming President," *Public Opinion Quarterly*, Vol. XXIII (Fall, 1959), pp. 361-70.

Hesseltine, William B. and Wolf, Hazel C. "The Cleveland Conference of 1861," *Ohio State Archaeological and Historical Quarterly*, Vol. LVI (July, 1947), pp. 258-65.

Joint Conference of Representatives of Congress and the Governors' Conference. Proceedings, reported as separate articles. *State Government*, Vol. XX (November, 1947), pp. 282-99.

Kallenbach, Joseph E. "Governors and the Presidency," *Michigan Alumnus Quarterly Review*, Vol. LX (Spring, 1954), pp. 234-42.

Lipson, Leslie. "The Executive Branch in New State Constitutions," *Public Administration Review*, Vol. IX (Winter, 1949), pp. 11-21.

Macdonald, Austin F. "American Governors," *National Municipal Review*, Vol. XVI (November, 1927), pp. 715-19.

MacKaye, Milton. "When Governors Get Together," *Saturday Evening Post*, May 10, 1958, pp. 32-33, 113-14.

Merriam, Charles E. "Observations on Centralization and Decentralization," *State Government*, Vol. XVI (January, 1943), pp. 3-5, 18.

———. "State Government at Mid-Century," *State Government*, Vol. XXIII (June, 1950), pp. 114-18.

Moos, Malcolm. "New Light on the Nominating Process," in Stephen K. Bailey, *et al. Research Frontiers in Politics and Government*. Brookings Lectures, 1955. Washington: The Brookings Institution, 1955, pp. 135-67.

Nixon, H. C. "The Southern Governors' Conference as a Pressure Group," *Journal of Politics*, Vol. VI (August, 1944), pp. 338-45.

Perkins, John A. "American Governors—1930 to 1940," *National Municipal Review*, Vol. XXIX (March, 1940), pp. 178-84.

"Political Rites," *Economist*, August 27, 1955, pp. 695-96.

Solomon, Samuel R. "American Governors Since 1915," *National Municipal Review*, Vol. XX (March, 1931), pp. 152–58.

Spicer, George W. "Gubernatorial Leadership in Virginia," *Public Administration Review*, Vol. I (Autumn, 1941), pp. 441–57.

Stevenson, Adlai E. "The States, the Federal System, and the People," *State Government*, Vol. XXIII (February, 1950), pp. 24–27, 40.

Stokes, Thomas L. "The Governors," *State Government*, Vol. XVII (June, 1944), pp. 343–46.

Stratton, William G. "The Governors' Conference Through Fifty Years—and Tomorrow," *State Government*, Vol. XXXI (Summer, 1958), 125–26.

Summaries of the annual Governors' Conferences. *State Government*, Vol. VIII–XXXIII (1935 through 1960).

Symposium. "Are We Maintaining Our Federal System?" *State Government*, Vol. XXII (January, 1949), supplement.

Toll, Henry W. "The Founding of the Council of State Governments," *State Government*, Vol. XXXII (Summer, 1959), pp. 162–64.

———. "Four Chapters Concerning the Council of State Governments," *State Government*, Vol. XI (November, 1938), pp. 199–205.

"War Powers of Governors." *State Government*, Vol. XV (February, 1942), pp. 39–40, 46–47.

White, Leonard D. and Sherman, M. Harvey. "The Governors March On," *State Government*, Vol. XIII (October, 1940), pp. 195–97, 206.

Young, William H. "The Development of the Governorship," *State Government*, Vol. XXXI (Summer, 1958), pp. 178–83.

Zimmerman, Frederick L. "Fourteen Creative Years," *State Government*, Vol. XXXII (Summer, 1959), pp. 164–73.

Public Documents

U.S. Commission on Intergovernmental Relations. Vol. I: *Report*. Washington: Government Printing Office, June, 1955.

———. Vol. VII: *A Study Committee Report on Unemployment Compensation and Employment Service*. Washington: Government Printing Office, June, 1955.

———. Vol. XII: *A Staff Report on Civil Defense and Urban Vulnerability*. Washington: Government Printing Office, June, 1955.

———. Vol. XIII: *A Staff Report on Federal Aid to Airports*. Washington: Government Printing Office, June, 1955.

U.S. Commission on Organization of the Executive Branch of the Government. *Overseas Administration, Federal-State Relations, Federal Research*. Washington: Government Printing Office, 1949, pp. 19–39.

U.S. Congress, House, Committee on Government Operations. *Establishing an*

Advisory Commission on Intergovernmental Relations. 86 Cong., 1 sess.,
House Report No. 742.

———. *Federal-State-Local Relations, Federal Grants-In-Aid, Thirtieth Report.*
85 Cong., 2 sess., House Report No. 2533.

———. *Hearings, Civil Defense for National Survival.* 84 Cong., 2 sess., May 4—
June 27, 1956.

U.S. Congress, House, Committee on Public Works. *Hearings, National Highway
Program, H.R. 4260.* 84 Cong., 1 sess., Part 1, April 18—June 1, 1955.

U.S. Congress, House, Committee on Ways and Means. *Hearings, Unemployment Compensation Act of 1945, H.R. 3736.* 79 Cong., 1 sess., August 30—
September 7, 1945.

———. *War Displacement Benefits, Hearings on H.R. 6559.* 77 Cong., 2 sess.,
February 11–17, 1942.

U.S. Congress, House, Committee on Ways and Means, Subcommittee on Coordination of Federal, State, and Local Taxes. *Report No. 2519.* 82 Cong., 2
sess., 1952.

U.S. Congress, House, Intergovernmental Relations Subcommittee and Senate,
Committee on Government Operations. *To Establish an Advisory Commission
on Intergovernmental Relations, Joint Hearings, H.R. 6904, H.R. 6905, and
S. 2026.* 86 Cong., 1 sess., June 16–22, 1959.

U.S. Congress, Senate, Committee on Armed Services, Subcommittee on Civil
Defense. *Hearings, Civil Defense Program.* 84 Cong., 1 sess., March 9—June
20, 1955.

U.S. Congress, Senate, Committee on Commerce, Subcommittee. *Hearings, Federal
Aid for Public Airports.* 79 Cong., 1 sess., March 13–23, 1945.

U.S. Congress, Senate, Committee on Finance. *Hearings, Emergency Unemployment Compensation, S. 1274.,* 79 Cong., 1 sess., August 29—September 4, 1945.

U.S. Congress, Senate, Committee on Public Works, Subcommittee. *Hearings,
National Highway Program, S. 1048, S. 1072, S. 1160, and S. 1573.* 84 Cong., 1
sess., February 21—April 15, 1955.

U.S. Department of Commerce, Bureau of Public Roads. *The Administration
of Federal Aid for Highways and Other Activities of the Bureau of Public
Roads.* Washington, 1957.

U.S. Department of Treasury, Committee on Intergovernmental Fiscal Relations. *Federal, State, and Local Government Fiscal Relations.* Printed as
Senate Document 69, 78 Cong., 1 sess., June 23, 1943.

Newspapers

Baltimore Sun.
Denver Post
New York Herald Tribune.
New York Times.
Washington Post and Times Herald.

Index

179